The War of Independ
By John Fiske

PREFACE.

This little book does not contain the substance of the lectures on the American Revolution which I have delivered in so many parts of the United States since 1883. Those lectures, when completed and published, will make quite a detailed narrative; this book is but a sketch. It is hoped that it may prove useful to the higher classes in schools, as well as to teachers. When I was a boy I should have been glad to get hold of a brief account of the War for Independence that would have suggested answers to some of the questions that used to vex me. Was the conduct of the British government, in driving the Americans into rebellion, merely wanton aggression, or was it not rather a bungling attempt to solve a political problem which really needed to be solved? Why were New Jersey and the Hudson river so important? Why did the British armies make South Carolina their chief objective point after New York? Or how did Cornwallis happen to be at Yorktown when Washington made such a long leap and pounced upon him there? And so on. Such questions the old-fashioned text-books not only did not try to answer, they did not even recognize their existence. As to the large histories, they of course include so many details that it requires maturity of judgment to discriminate between the facts that are cardinal and those that are merely incidental. When I give lectures to schoolboys and schoolgirls, I observe that a reference to causes and effects always seems to heighten the interest of the story. I therefore offer them this little book, not as a rival but as an aid to the ordinary text-book. I am aware that a narrative so condensed must necessarily suffer from the omission of many picturesque and striking details. The world is so made that one often has to lose a little in one direction in order to gain something in another. This book is an experiment. If it seems to answer its purpose, I may follow it with others, treating other portions of American history in similar fashion.

CAMBRIDGE, *February 11, 1889.*

BIOGRAPHICAL SKETCH.

To relate, by way of leading up to this little book, all the previous achievements of its author would--without disrespect to the greater or the less--have somewhat the appearance of putting a very big cart in front of a pony. But no idea could be more mistaken than that which induces people to believe a small book the easiest to write. Easy reading is hard writing; and a thoroughly good small book stands for so much more than the mere process of putting it on paper, that its value is not at all to be judged by its bulk. The offhand word of a man full of knowledge is worth a great deal more than the carefully prepared utterance of a person who having spoken once has nothing more to say. In our introduction to this work, therefore, we propose to reverse the common process of tracing the author's development upwards, and instead, after stating the mere events of Mr. Fiske's life, to begin with "The War of Independence" and to follow his work backwards, attempting very briefly to show how each undertaking was built naturally upon something before it, and that the original basis of the structure was uncommonly broad and strong.

John Fiske was born in Hartford, Conn., 30th March, 1842, and spent most of his life, before entering Harvard as a sophomore in 1860, with his grandmother's family in Middletown, Conn. Two years after taking his degree at Harvard, in 1863, he was graduated from the Harvard Law School, but he cared so much more for writing than for the law that his attempt to practice it in

Boston was soon abandoned. In 1861 he made his first important contribution to a magazine, and ever since has done much work of the same sort. He has served Harvard College, as University lecturer on philosophy, 1869-71, in 1870 as instructor in history, and from 1872 to 1879 as assistant librarian. Since resigning from that office he has been for two terms of six years each a member of the board of overseers. In 1881 he began lecturing annually at Washington University, St. Louis, on American history, and in 1884 was made a professor of the institution. Since 1871 he has devoted much time to lecturing at large. He has been heard in most of the principal cities of America, and abroad, in London and Edinburgh. All this time his home has been in Cambridge, Mass.

So much for the simple outward circumstances of Mr. Fiske's life. Turning to his studies and writings, one finds them reaching out into almost every direction of human thought; and this book, from which our backward course is to be taken, is but a page from the great body of his work. It is especially as a student of philosophy, science, and history that Mr. Fiske is known to the world; and at the present it is particularly as an historian of America that his name is spoken. In no other way more satisfactorily than in tracing the growth of his own nation has he found it possible to study the laws of progress of the human race, and from the first, through all the time of his most active philosophical and scientific work, this study of human progress has been the true interest of his life. With his historical works, then, let us begin.

In 1879 he delivered a course of six lectures on American history, at the Old South Meeting House in Boston. In previous years he had written occasional essays on historical subjects in general, but the impulse towards American history in particular was given by the preparation for these lectures, which were concerned especially with the colonial period. Of his own treatment of an historical subject he is quoted as saying: "I look it up or investigate it, and then write an essay or a lecture on the subject. That serves as a preliminary statement, either of a large subject or of special points. It is a help to me to make a statement of the kind--I mean in the lecture or essay form. In fact it always assists me to try to state the case. I never publish anything after this first statement, but generally keep it with me for, it may be, some years, and possibly return to it again several times." Thus it may safely be assumed that these Old South Lectures and the many others that have followed them have found or will find a permanent place in the series of Mr. Fiske's historical volumes.

The succession of these books has not been in the order of the periods of which they treat; but from the similarity of their method and the fact that they cover a series of important periods in American history, they go towards making a complete, consecutive history of the country. The periods which are not yet covered Mr. Fiske proposes to deal with in time. One who has talked with him on the subject of his works reports the following statement as coming from Mr. Fiske's own lips: "I am now at work on a general history of the United States. When John Richard Green was planning his 'Short History of the English People,' and he and I were friends in London, I heard him telling about his scheme. I thought it would be a very nice thing to do something of the same sort for American history. But when I took it up I found myself, instead of carrying it out in that way, dwelling upon special points; and insensibly, without any volition on my part, I suppose, it has been rather taking the shape of separate monographs. But I hope to go on in that way until I cover the ground with these separate books,--that is, to cover as much ground as possible. But, of course, the scheme has become much more extensive than it was when I started."

Taken in the order of their subjects, the five works already contributed to this series are, "The Discovery of America, with some Account of Ancient America and the Spanish Conquest" (two volumes); "Old Virginia and her Neighbours" (two volumes); "The Beginnings of New England, or the Puritan Theocracy in its Relations to Civil and Religious Liberty;" "The American Revolution" (two volumes); and "The Critical Period of American History, 1783-1789." Allied with these books, though hardly taking a place in the series, is "Civil Government in the United States, Considered with some Reference to its Origins," "The War of Independence," it will thus be seen, is the least ambitious of all these historical works. "A History of the United States for Schools" is addressed to the same audience, and in so far may be considered a companion volume.

What makes Mr. Fiske's histories just what they are? Another step backward in the stages of his own development will enable us to see, and the sub-title, "Viewed from the Standpoint of Universal History," of one of his earlier books, "American Political Ideas," will help towards an understanding of his power. It is due to the fact that he brings to his historical work on special subjects the broad philosophic and general view of a man who is much more than a specialist,-- the scientific habit of mind which must look for causes when effects are seen, and must point out the relations between them. There could be no better preparation for the writing of history than the apparently alien study of the questions with which the names of Darwin and Spencer are inseparably associated. When Darwin's "Origin of Species" appeared, Mr. Fiske's own thought had prepared him to take the place of an ardent apostle of Evolution, and it is held that no man has done more than he in expounding the theory in America. Standing permanently for his work in this field are his books, "Excursions of an Evolutionist" and "Darwinism, and Other Essays." One of his first important works was "Outlines of Cosmic Philosophy" (1874), and in more recent years "The Destiny of Man" and "The Idea of God" speak forth very distinctly, not as interpretations, but as his own contributions to the progress of philosophic thought. One other phase of the use to which Mr. Fiske's mind has been put should surely be mentioned in any summary of his qualifications for writing histories. He is extremely fond of hearing and telling good stories. His book on "Myths and Myth-makers" (1872) gave early evidence of this fondness, and surely there is the very spirit of the lover of tales in the Dedication of the book, "To my dear Friend, William D. Howells, in remembrance of pleasant autumn evenings spent among were-wolves and trolls and nixies." Thus, besides the ability to see a story in all its bearings, Mr. Fiske has the gift of telling it effectively,--a golden power without which all the learning in the world would serve an historian as but so much lead.

But all of these works preceding Mr. Fiske's historical writings did not come out of nothing. His mental acquirements as a young man and boy were very extraordinary, and give to the last stage of his career at which we shall look--the earliest--perhaps the greatest interest of all. A description of it without a knowledge of what followed would be all too apt to remind readers whose memories go back far enough of the instances, all too common, of men whose early promise is not fulfilled. *Summa cum laude* graduates settle down into lives of timid routine that leads to nothing, just as often as the idle dreamers who stay consistently at the foot of their classes wake up when the vital contact with the world takes place, and do something astonishingly good. These, however, are the exceptions. A development like Mr. Fiske's follows the lines of nature.

Happily, there were books in the house in which he was brought up. At the age of seven he was reading Rollin, Josephus, and Goldsmith's Greece. Much of Milton, Pope, and Bunyan, and nearly all of Shakespeare he had read before he was nine; histories of many lands before eleven. At this age he filled a quarto blank book of sixty pages with a chronological table, written from memory, of events between 1000 B. C. and 1820 A. D.

All this would seem enough for one boy, but there were the other worlds of languages and science to conquer. It is almost discouraging merely to write down the fact that at thirteen he had read a large part of Livy, Cicero, Ovid, Catullus, and Juvenal, and all of Virgil, Horace, Tacitus, Sallust, and Suetonius,--to say nothing of Cæsar, at seven. Greek was disposed of in like manner; and then came the modern languages, --German, Spanish,--in which he kept a diary,--French, Italian, and Portuguese. Hebrew and Sanskrit were kept for the years of seventeen and eighteen. In college, Icelandic, Gothic, Danish, Swedish, Dutch, and Roumanian were added, with beginnings in Russian. The uses to which he put these languages were not those to which the weary schoolboy puts his few scraps of learning in foreign tongues, but the true uses of literature,--reading for pleasure and mental stimulus.

It is needless to relate the rapid course of Mr. Fiske's first studies in science; it is no whit less remarkable than that of his other intellectual enterprises. As mathematics is akin to music, it will be enough to say that when he was fifteen a friend's piano was left in his grandmother's house, and, without a master, the boy soon learned its secrets well enough to play such works as Mozart's Twelfth Mass. Later in life Mr. Fiske studied the science of music. He has printed many musical criticisms, and has himself composed a mass and songs.

Few boys can hope to take to college with them, or, for that matter, even away from it, a mind so well equipped as Mr. Fiske's was when he went to Cambridge. Three years of stimulating university atmosphere, and of indefinitely wide opportunities for reading, left him prepared as few men have been for just the work he has done. He has had the wisdom to see what he could do, and being possessed of the qualities that lead to accomplishment, he has done it; and any reader who understands more than the mere words he reads will be very likely to discover in this small volume, "The War of Independence," something of the spirit, and some suggestions of the method which, in this sketch, we have endeavored to point out as characteristic of one of the foremost living historians.

THE WAR OF INDEPENDENCE.

CHAPTER I.INTRODUCTION.

Since the year 1875 we have witnessed, in many parts of the United States, public processions, meetings, and speeches in commemoration of the hundredth anniversary of some important event in the course of our struggle for national independence. This series of centennial celebrations, which has been of great value in stimulating American patriotism and awakening throughout the country a keen interest in American history, will naturally come to an end in 1889. The close of President Cleveland's term of office marks the close of the first century of the government under which we live, which dates from the inauguration of President Washington on the balcony of the

Federal building in Wall street, New York, on the 30th of April, 1789. It was on that memorable day that the American Revolution may be said to have been completed. The Declaration of Independence in 1776 detached the American people from the supreme government to which they had hitherto owed allegiance, and it was not until Washington's inauguration in 1789 that the supreme government to which we owe allegiance to-day was actually put in operation. The period of thirteen years included between these two dates was strictly a revolutionary period, during which it was more or less doubtful where the supreme authority over the United States belonged. First, it took the fighting and the diplomacy of the revolutionary war to decide that this supreme authority belonged in the United States themselves, and not in the government of Great Britain; and then after the war was ended, more than five years of sore distress and anxious discussion had elapsed before the American people succeeded in setting up a new government that was strong enough to make itself obeyed at home and respected abroad.

It is the story of this revolutionary period, ending in 1789, that we have here to relate in its principal outlines. When we stand upon the crest of a lofty hill and look about in all directions over the landscape, we can often detect relations between distant points which we had not before thought of together. While we tarried in the lowland, we could see blue peaks rising here and there against the sky, and follow babbling brooks hither and thither through the forest. It was more homelike down there than on the hilltop, for in each gnarled tree, in every moss-grown boulder, in every wayside flower, we had a friend that was near to us; but the general bearings of things may well have escaped our notice. In climbing to our lonely vantage-ground, while the familiar scenes fade from sight, there are gradually unfolded to us those connections between crag and meadow and stream that make the life and meaning of the whole. We learn the "lay of the land," and become, in a humble way, geographers. So in the history of men and nations, while we remain immersed in the study of personal incidents and details, as what such a statesman said or how many men were killed in such a battle, we may quite fail to understand what it was all about, and we shall be sure often to misjudge men's characters and estimate wrongly the importance of many events. For this reason we cannot clearly see the meaning of the history of our own times. The facts are too near us; we are down among them, like the man who could not see the forest because there were so many trees. But when we look back over a long interval of years, we can survey distant events and personages like points in a vast landscape and begin to discern the meaning of it all. In this way we come to see that history is full of lessons for us. Very few things have happened in past ages with which our present welfare is not in one way or another concerned. Few things have happened in any age more interesting or more important than the American Revolution.

CHAPTER II. THE COLONIES IN 1750.

It is always difficult in history to mark the beginning and end of a period. Events keep rushing on and do not pause to be divided into chapters; or, in other words, in the history which really takes place, a new chapter is always beginning long before the old one is ended. The divisions we make when we try to describe it are merely marks that we make for our own convenience. In telling the story of the American Revolution we must stop somewhere, and the inauguration of President Washington is a very proper place. We must also begin somewhere, but it is quite clear that it will not do to begin with the Declaration of Independence in July, 1776, or even with the midnight ride of Paul Revere in April, 1775. For if we ask what caused that "hurry of hoofs in a village street," and what brought together those five-and-fifty statesmen at Philadelphia, we are not simply led back to the Boston Tea-Party, and still further to the Stamp Act, but we find it necessary to refer to events that happened more than a century before the Revolution can properly be said to have begun. Indeed, if we were going to take a very wide view of the situation, and try to point out its relations to the general history of mankind, we should have to go back many hundreds of years and not only cross the ocean to the England of King Alfred, but keep on still further to the ancient market-places of Rome and Athens, and even to the pyramids of Egypt; and in all this long journey through the ages we should not be merely gratifying an idle curiosity, but at every step of the way could gather sound practical lessons, useful in helping us to vote intelligently at the next election for mayor of the city in which we live or for president of the United States.

[Sidenote: The half-way station in American History]

We are not now, however, about to start on any such long journey. It is a much nearer and narrower view of the American Revolution that we wish to get. There are many points from which we might start, but we must at any rate choose a point several years earlier than the Declaration of Independence. People are very apt to leave out of sight the "good old colony times" and speak of our country as scarcely more than a hundred years old. Sometimes we hear the presidency of George Washington spoken of as part of "early American history;" but we ought not to forget that when Washington was born the commonwealth of Virginia was already one hundred and twenty-five years old. The first governor of Massachusetts was born three centuries ago, in 1588, the year of the Spanish Armada. Suppose we take the period of 282 years between the English settlement of Virginia and the inauguration of President Benjamin Harrison, and divide it in the middle. That gives us the year 1748 as the half-way station in the history of the American people. There were just as many years of continuous American history before 1748 as there have been since that date. That year was famous for the treaty of Aix-la-Chapelle, which put an end to a war between England and France that had lasted five years. That war had been waged in America as well as in Europe, and American troops had played a brilliant part in it. There was now a brief lull, soon to be followed by another and greater war between the two mighty rivals, and it was in the course of this latter war that some of the questions were raised which presently led to the American Revolution. Let us take the occasion of this lull in the storm to look over the American world and see what were the circumstances likely to lead to the throwing off of the British government by the thirteen colonies, and to their union under a federal government of their own making.

[Sidenote: The four New England colonies.]

In the middle of the eighteenth century there were four New England colonies. Massachusetts extended her sway over Maine, and the Green Mountain territory was an uninhabited wilderness, to which New York and New Hampshire alike laid claim. The four commonwealths of New Hampshire, Massachusetts, Connecticut, and Rhode Island had all been in existence, under one form or another, for more than a century. The men who were in the prime of life there in 1750 were the great-grandsons and great-great-grandsons of the men who crossed the ocean between 1620 and 1640 and settled New England. Scarcely two men in a hundred were of other than English blood. About one in a hundred could say that his family came from Scotland or the north of Ireland; one in five hundred may have been the grandchild of a Huguenot. Upon religious and political questions these people thought very much alike. Extreme poverty was almost unknown, and there were but few who could not read and write. As a rule every head of a family owned the house in which he lived and the land which supported him. There were no cities; and from Boston, which was a town with 16,000 inhabitants, down to the smallest settlement in the White Mountains, the government was carried on by town-meetings at which, almost any grown-up man could be present and speak and vote. Except upon the sea-coast nearly all the people lived upon farms; but all along the coast were many who lived by fishing and by building ships, and in the towns dwelt many merchants grown rich by foreign trade. In those days Massachusetts was the richest of the thirteen colonies, and had a larger population than any other except Virginia. Connecticut was then more populous than New York; and when the four New England commonwealths acted together--as was likely to be the case in time of danger--they formed the strongest military power on the American continent.

[Sidenote: Virginia and Maryland]

Among what we now call southern states there were two that in 1750 were more than a hundred years old. These were Virginia and Maryland. The people of these commonwealths, like those of New England, had lived together in America long enough to become distinctively Americans. Both New Englander and Virginian had had time to forget their family relationships with the kindred left behind so long ago in England; though there were many who did not forget it, and in our time scholars have by research recovered many of the links that had been lost from memory. The white people of Virginia were as purely English as those of Connecticut or Massachusetts. But society in Virginia was very different from society in New England. The wealth of Virginia consisted chiefly of tobacco, which was raised by negro slaves. People lived far apart from each other on great plantations, usually situated near the navigable streams of which that country has so many. Most of the great planters had easy access to private wharves, where their crops could be loaded on ships and sent directly to England in exchange for all sorts of goods. Accordingly it was but seldom that towns grew up as centres of trade. Each plantation was a kind of little world in itself. There were no town-meetings, as the smallest political division was the division into counties; but there were county-meetings quite vigorous with political life. Of the leading county families a great many were descended from able and distinguished Cavaliers or King's-men who had come over from England during the ascendency of Oliver Cromwell. Skill in the management of public affairs was hereditary in such families, and during our revolutionary period Virginia produced more great leaders than any of the other colonies.

[Sidenote: New York and Delaware]

There were yet two other American commonwealths that in 1750 were more than a hundred years old. These were New York and little Delaware, which for some time was a kind of appendage, first to New York, afterward to Pennsylvania. But there was one important respect in which these two colonies were different alike from New England and from Virginia. Their population was far from being purely English. Delaware had been first settled by Swedes, New York by Dutchmen; and the latter colony had drawn its settlers from almost every part of western and central Europe. A man might travel from Penobscot bay to the Harlem river without hearing a syllable in any other tongue than English; but in crossing Manhattan island he could listen, if he chose, to more than a dozen languages. There was almost as much diversity in opinions about religious and political matters as there was in the languages in which they were expressed. New York was an English community in so far as it had been for more than eighty years under an English government, but hardly in any other sense. Accordingly we shall find New York in the revolutionary period less prompt and decided in action than Massachusetts and Virginia. In population New York ranked only seventh among the thirteen colonies; but in its geographical position it was the most important of all. It was important commercially because the Mohawk and Hudson rivers formed a direct avenue for the fur-trade from the region of the great lakes to the finest harbour on all the Atlantic coast. In a military sense it was important for two reasons; *first*, because the Mohawk valley was the home of the most powerful confederacy of Indians on the continent, the steady allies of the English and deadly foes of the French; *secondly*, because the centre of the French power was at Montreal and Quebec, and from those points the route by which the English colonies could be most easily invaded was formed by Lake Champlain and the Hudson river. New York was completely interposed between New England and the rest of the English colonies, so that an enemy holding possession of it would virtually cut the Atlantic seaboard in two. For these reasons the political action of New York was of most critical importance.

[Sidenote: The two Carolinas and Georgia; New Jersey and Pennsylvania]

Of the other colonies in 1750, the two Carolinas and New Jersey were rather more than eighty years old, while Pennsylvania had been settled scarcely seventy years. But the growth of these younger colonies had been rapid, especially in the case of Pennsylvania and North Carolina, which in populousness ranked third and fourth among the thirteen. This rapid increase was mainly due to a large immigration from Europe kept up during the first half of the eighteenth century, so that a large proportion of the people had either been born in Europe, or were the children of people born in Europe. In 1750 these colonies had not had time enough to become so intensely American as Virginia and the New England colonies. In Georgia, which had been settled only seventeen years, people had had barely time to get used to this new home on the wild frontier.

The population of these younger colonies was very much mixed. In South Carolina, as in New York, probably less than half were English. In both Carolinas there were a great many Huguenots from France, and immigrants from Germany and Scotland and the north of Ireland were still pouring in. Pennsylvania had many Germans and Irish, and settlers from other parts of Europe, besides its English Quakers. With all this diversity of race there was a great diversity of opinions about political questions, as about other matters.

[Sidenote: Why Massachusetts and Virginia took the lead.]

We are now beginning to see why it was that Massachusetts and Virginia took the lead in bringing on the revolutionary war. Not only were these two the largest colonies, but their people had become much more thoroughly welded together in their thoughts and habits and associations than was as yet possible with the people of the younger colonies. When the revolutionary war came, there were very few Tories in the New England colonies and very few in Virginia; but there were a great many in New York and Pennsylvania and the two Carolinas, so that the action of these commonwealths was often slow and undecided, and sometimes there was bitter and bloody fighting between men of opposite opinions, especially in New York and South Carolina.

[Sidenote: The two republics; Connecticut and Rhode Island]

If we look at the governments of the thirteen colonies in the middle of the eighteenth century, we shall observe some interesting facts. All the colonies had legislative assemblies elected by the people, and these assemblies levied the taxes and made the laws. So far as the legislatures were concerned, therefore, all the colonies governed themselves. But with regard to the executive department of the government, there were very important differences. Only two of the colonies, Connecticut and Rhode Island, had governors elected by the people. These two colonies were completely self-governing. In almost everything but name they were independent of Great Britain, and this was so true that at the time of the revolutionary war they did not need to make any new constitutions for themselves, but continued to live on under their old charters for many years,--Connecticut until 1818, Rhode Island until 1843. Before the revolution these two colonies had comparatively few direct grievances to complain of at the hands of Great Britain; but as they were next neighbours to Massachusetts and closely connected with its history, they were likely to sympathize promptly with the kind of grievances by which Massachusetts was disturbed.

[Sidenote: The proprietary governments: Pennsylvania, Delaware, and Maryland]

Three of the colonies, Pennsylvania, Delaware, and Maryland, had a peculiar kind of government, known as *proprietary government*. Their territories had originally been granted by the crown to a person known as the Lord Proprietary, and the lord-proprietorship descended from father to son like a kingdom. In Maryland it was the Calvert family that reigned for six generations as lords proprietary. Pennsylvania and Delaware had each its own separate legislature, but over both colonies reigned the same lord proprietary, who was a member of the Penn family. These colonies were thus like little hereditary monarchies, and they had but few direct dealings with the British government. For them the lords proprietary stood in the place of the king, and appointed the governors. In Maryland this system ran smoothly. In Pennsylvania there was a good deal of dissatisfaction, but it generally assumed the form of a wish to get rid of the lords proprietary and have the governors appointed by the king; for as this was something they had not tried they were not prepared to appreciate its evils.

[Sidenote: The crown colonies and their royal governors]

In the other eight colonies--New Hampshire, Massachusetts, New York, New Jersey, Virginia, the two Carolinas, and Georgia--the governors were appointed by the king, and were commonly known as "royal governors." They were sometimes natives of the colonies over which they were appointed, as Dudley and Hutchinson of Massachusetts, and others; but were more often sent over from England. Some of them, as Pownall of Massachusetts and Spotswood of Virginia, were men of marked ability. Some were honest gentlemen, who felt a real interest in the welfare of the people they came to help govern; some were unprincipled adventurers, who came to make money by fair means or foul. Their position was one of much dignity, and they behaved themselves like lesser kings. What with their crimson velvets and fine laces and stately coaches, they made much more of a show than any president of the United States would think of making to-day. They had no fixed terms of office, but remained at their posts as long as the king, or the king's colonial secretary, saw fit to keep them there.

[Sidenote: The question as to salaries]

Now it was generally true of the royal governors that, whether they were natives of America or sent over from England, and whether they were good men or bad, they were very apt to make themselves disliked by the people, and they were almost always quarrelling with their legislative assemblies. Questions were always coming up about which the governor and the legislature could not agree, because the legislature represented the views of the people who had chosen it, while the governor represented his own views or the views which prevailed three thousand miles away among the king's ministers, who very often knew little about America and cared less. One of these disputed questions related to the governor's salary. It was natural that the governor should wish to have a salary of fixed amount, so that he might know from year to year what he was going to receive. But the people were afraid that if this were to be done the governor might become too independent. They preferred that the legislature should each year make a grant of money such as it should deem suitable for the governor's expenses, and this sum it might increase or diminish according to its own good pleasure. This would keep the governor properly subservient to the legislature. Before 1750 there had been much bitter wrangling over this question in several of the colonies, and the governors had one after another been obliged to submit, though with very ill grace.

Sometimes the thoughts of the royal governors and their friends went beyond this immediate question. Since the legislatures were so froward and so niggardly, what an admirable plan it would be to have the governors paid out of the royal treasury and thus made comparatively independent of the legislatures! The judges, too, who were quite poorly paid, might fare much better if remunerated by the crown, and the same might be said of some other public officers. But if the British government were to undertake to pay the salaries of its officials in America, it must raise a revenue for the purpose; and it would naturally raise such a revenue by levying taxes in America rather than in England. People in England felt that they were already taxed as heavily as they could bear, in order to pay the expenses of their own government. They could not be expected to submit to further taxation for the sake of paying the expenses of governing the American colonies. If further taxes were to be laid for such a purpose, they must in fairness be laid upon Americans, not upon Englishmen in the old country.

Such was the view which people in England would naturally be expected to take, and such was the view which they generally did take. But there was another side to the question which was very clearly seen by most people in America. If the royal governors were to be paid by the crown and thus made independent of their legislatures, there would be danger of their becoming petty tyrants and interfering in many ways with the liberties of the people. Still greater would be the danger if the judges were to be paid by the crown, for then they would feel themselves responsible to the king or to the royal governor, rather than to their fellow-citizens; and it would be easy for the governors, by appointing corrupt men as judges, to prevent the proper administration of justice by the courts, and thus to make men's lives and property insecure. Most Americans in 1750 felt this danger very keenly. They had not forgotten how, in the times of their grandfathers, two of the noblest of Englishmen, Lord William Russell and Colonel Algernon

Sidney, had been murdered by the iniquitous sentence of time-serving judges. They had not forgotten the ruffian George Jeffreys and his "bloody assizes" of 1685. They well remembered how their kinsmen in England had driven into exile the Stuart family of kings, who were even yet, in 1745, making efforts to recover their lost throne. They remembered how the beginnings of New England had been made by stout-hearted men who could not endure the tyranny of these same Stuarts; and they knew well that one of the worst of the evils upon which Stuart tyranny had fattened had been the corruption of the courts of justice. The Americans believed with some reason, that even now, in the middle of the eighteenth century, the administration of justice in their own commonwealths was decidedly better than in Great Britain; and they had no mind to have it disturbed.

[Sidenote: "No taxation without representation."]

But worse than all, if the expenses of governing America were to be paid by taxes levied upon Americans and collected from them by king or parliament or any power whatsoever residing in Great Britain, then the inhabitants of the thirteen American colonies would at once cease to be free people. A free country is one in which the government cannot take away people's money, in the shape of taxes, except for strictly public purposes and with the consent of the people themselves, as expressed by some body of representatives whom the people have chosen. If people's money can be taken from them without their consent, no matter how small the amount, even if it be less than one dollar out of every thousand, then they are not politically free. They do not govern, but the power that thus takes their money without their consent is the power that governs; and there is nothing to prevent such a power from using the money thus obtained to strengthen itself until it can trample upon people's rights in every direction, and rob them of their homes and lives as well as of their money. If the British government could tax the Americans without their consent, it might use the money for supporting a British army in America, and such an army might be employed in intimidating the legislatures, in dispersing town-meetings, in destroying newspaper-offices, or in other acts of tyranny.

[Sidenote: It was the fundamental principle of English liberty.]

The Americans in the middle of the eighteenth century well understood that the principle of "no taxation without representation" is the fundamental principle of free government. It was the principle for which their forefathers had contended again and again in England, and upon which the noble edifice of English liberty had been raised and consolidated since the grand struggle between king and barons in the thirteenth century. It had passed into a tradition, both in England and in America, that in order to prevent the crown from becoming despotic, it was necessary that it should only wield such revenues as the representatives of the people might be pleased to grant it. In England the body which represented the people was the House of Commons, in each of the American colonies it was the colonial legislature; and in dealing with the royal governors, the legislatures acted upon the same general principles as the House of Commons in dealing with the king.

[Sidenote: Sometimes the royal governors were in the right, as to the particular question.]

It was not until some time after 1750 that any grand assault was made upon the principle of "no taxation without representation," but the frequent disputes with the royal governors were such as to keep people from losing sight of this principle, and to make them sensitive about acts that might lead to violations of it. In the particular disputes the governors were sometimes clearly right and the people wrong. One of the principal objects, as we shall presently see, for which the governors wanted money, was to maintain troops for defence against the French and the Indians; and the legislatures were apt to be short-sighted and unreasonably stingy about such matters. Again, the people were sometimes seized with a silly craze for "paper money" and "wild-cat banks"--devices for making money out of nothing--and sometimes the governors were sensible enough to oppose such delusions but not altogether sensible in their manner of doing it. Thus in 1740 there was fierce excitement in Massachusetts over a quarrel between the governor and the legislature about the famous "silver bank" and "land bank." These institutions were a public nuisance and deserved to be suppressed, but the governor was obliged to appeal to parliament in order to succeed in doing it. This led many people to ask, "What business has a parliament sitting the other side of the ocean to be making laws for us?" and the grumbling was loud and bitter enough to show that this was a very dangerous question to raise.

[Sidenote: Bitter memories; in Virginia.]

It was in the eight colonies which had royal governors that troubles of a revolutionary character were more likely to arise than in the other five, but there were special reasons, besides those already mentioned, why Massachusetts and Virginia should prove more refractory than any of the others. Both these great commonwealths had bitter memories. Things had happened in both which might serve as a warning, and which some of the old men still living in 1750 could distinctly remember. In Virginia the misgovernment of the royal governor Sir William Berkeley had led in 1675 to the famous rebellion headed by Nathaniel Bacon, and this rebellion had been suppressed with much harshness. Many leading citizens had been sent to the gallows and their estates had been confiscated. In Massachusetts, though there were no such scenes of cruelty to remember, the grievance was much more deep-seated and enduring.

[Sidenote: And in Massachusetts.]

Massachusetts had not been originally a royal province, with its governors appointed by the king. At first it had been a republic, such as Connecticut and Rhode Island now were, with governors chosen by the people. From its foundation in 1629 down to 1684 the commonwealth of Massachusetts had managed its own affairs at its own good pleasure. Practically it had been not only self-governing but almost independent. That was because affairs in England were in such confusion that until after 1660 comparatively little attention was paid to what was going on in America, and the liberties of Massachusetts prospered through the neglect of what was then called the "home government." After Charles II. came to the throne in 1660 he began to interfere with the affairs of Massachusetts, and so the very first generation of men that had been born on the soil of that commonwealth were engaged in a long struggle against the British king for the right of managing their own affairs. After more than twenty years of this struggle, which by 1675 had come to be quite bitter, the charter of Massachusetts was annulled in 1684 and its free government was for the moment destroyed. Presently a viceroy was sent over from England, to govern Massachusetts (as well as several other northern colonies) despotically. This viceroy, Sir Edmund Andros, seems to have been a fairly well meaning man. He was not especially harsh or cruel, but his rule was a despotism, because he was not responsible to the people for what he did, but only to the king. In point of fact the two-and-a-half years of his administration were characterized by arbitrary arrests and by interference with private property and with the freedom of the press. It was so vexatious that early in 1689, taking advantage of the Revolution then going on in England, the people of Boston rose in rebellion, seized Andros and threw him into jail, and set up for themselves a provisional government. When the affairs of New England were settled after the accession of William and Mary to the throne, Connecticut and Rhode Island were allowed to keep their old governments; but Massachusetts in 1693 was obliged to take a new charter instead of her old one, and although this new charter revived the election of legislatures by the people, it left the governors henceforth to be appointed by the king.

In the political controversies of Massachusetts, therefore, in the eighteenth century, the people were animated by the recollection of what they had lost. They were somewhat less free and independent than their grandfathers had been, and they had learned what it was to have an irresponsible ruler sitting at his desk in Boston and signing warrants for the arrest of loved and respected citizens who dared criticise his sayings and doings. "Taxation without representation" was not for them a mere abstract theory; they knew what it meant. It was as near to them as the presidency of Andrew Jackson is to us; there had not been time enough to forget it. In every contest between the popular legislature and the royal governor there was some broad principle involved which there were plenty of well-remembered facts to illustrate.

[Sidenote: Grounds of sympathy between Massachusetts and Virginia.]

These contests also helped to arouse a strong sympathy between the popular leaders in Massachusetts and in Virginia. Between the people of the two colonies there was not much real sympathy, because there was a good deal of difference between their ways of life and their opinions about things; and people, unless they are unusually wise and generous of nature, are apt to dislike and despise those who differ from them in opinions and habits. So there was little cordiality of feeling between the people of Massachusetts and the people of Virginia, but in spite of this there was a great and growing political sympathy. This was because, ever since 1693, they had been obliged to deal with the same kind of political questions. It became intensely interesting to a Virginian to watch the progress of a dispute between the governor and legislature of Massachusetts, because whatever principle might be victorious in the course of such a dispute, it was sure soon to find a practical application in Virginia. Hence by the middle of the eighteenth century the two colonies were keenly observant of each other, and either one was exceedingly prompt in taking its cue from the other. It is worth while to remember this fact, for without it there would doubtless have been rebellions or revolutions of American colonies, but there would hardly have been one American Revolution, ending in a grand American Union.

CHAPTER III.THE FRENCH WARS, AND THE FIRST PLAN OF UNION.

[Sidenote: Disputed frontier between French and English colonies.]

It was said a moment ago that one of the chief objects for which the governors wanted money was to maintain troops for defence against the French and the Indians. This was a very serious matter indeed. To any one who looked at a map of North America in 1750 it might well have seemed as if the French had secured for themselves the greater part of the continent. The western frontier of the English settlements was generally within two hundred miles of the sea-coast. In New York it was at Johnson Hall, not far from Schenectady; in Pennsylvania it was about at Carlisle; in Virginia it was near Winchester, and the first explorers were just making their way across the Alleghany mountains. Westward of these frontier settlements lay endless stretches of forest inhabited by warlike tribes of red men who, everywhere except in New York, were hostile to the English and friendly to the French. Since the beginning of the seventeenth century French towns and villages had been growing up along the St. Lawrence, and French explorers had been pushing across the Great Lakes and down the valley of the Mississippi river, near the mouth of which the French town of New Orleans had been standing since 1718. It was the French doctrine that discovery and possession of a river gave a claim to all the territory drained by that river. According to this doctrine every acre of American soil from which water flowed into the St. Lawrence and the Mississippi belonged to France. The claims of the French thus came up to the very crest of the Alleghanies, and they made no secret of their intention to shut up the English forever between that chain of mountains and the sea-coast. There were times when their aims were still more aggressive and dangerous, when they looked with longing eyes upon the valley of the Hudson, and would fain have broken through that military centre of the line of English commonwealths and seized the keys of empire over the continent.

[Sidenote: The Indian tribes.]

From this height of their ambition the French were kept aloof by the deadly enmity of the most fierce and powerful savages in the New World. The Indians of those days who came into contact with the white settlers were divided into many tribes with different names, but they all belonged to one or another of three great stocks or families. First, there were the *Mobilians*, far down south; to this stock belonged the Creeks, Cherokees, and others. Secondly, there were the *Algonquins*, comprising the Delawares to the south of the Susquehanna; the Miamis, Shawnees, and others in the western wilderness; the Ottawas in Canada; and all the tribes still left to the northeast of New England. Thirdly, there were the *Iroquois*, of whom the most famous were the Five Nations of what is now central New York. These five great tribes--the Mohawks, Oneidas, Onondagas, Cayugas, and Senecas--had for several generations been united in a confederacy which they likened to a long wigwam with its eastern door looking out upon the valley of the Hudson and its western toward the falls of Niagara. It was known far and wide over the continent as the Long House, and wherever it was known it was dreaded. When Frenchmen and Englishmen first settled in America, this Iroquois league was engaged in a long career of conquest. Algonquin tribes all the way from the Connecticut to the Mississippi were treated as its vassals and forced to pay tribute in weapons and wampum. This conquering career extended through the seventeenth century, until it was brought to an end by the French. When the latter began making settlements in Canada, they courted the friendship of their Algonquin neighbours, and thus, without dreaming what deadly seed they were sowing, they were led to attack the terrible Long House. It was easy enough for Champlain in 1609 to win a victory over savages who had never before seen a white man or heard the report of a musket; but the victory was a fatal one for the French, for it made the Iroquois their eternal enemies. The Long House allied itself first with the Dutch and afterwards with the English, and thus checked the progress of the French toward the lower Hudson. We too seldom think how much we owe to those formidable savages.

[Sidenote: The French and the Iroquois.]

The Iroquois pressed the French with so much vigour that in 1689 they even laid siege to Montreal. But by 1696 the French, assisted by all the Algonquin tribes within reach, and led by their warlike viceroy, Count Frontenac, one of the most picturesque figures in American history, at length succeeded in getting the upperhand and dealing the Long House a terrible blow, from the effects of which it never recovered. The league remained formidable, however, until the time of the revolutionary war. In 1715 its fighting strength was partially repaired by the adoption of the kindred Iroquois tribe of Tuscaroras, who had just been expelled from North Carolina by the English settlers, and migrated to New York. After this accession the league, henceforth known as the Six Nations, formed a power by no means to be despised, though much less bold and aggressive than in the previous century.

After administering a check to the Iroquois, the French and Algonquins kept up for more than sixty years a desultory warfare against the English colonies. Whenever war broke out between England and France, it meant war in America as well as in Europe. Indeed, one of the chief objects of war, on the part of each of these two nations, was to extend its colonial dominions at the expense of the other. France and England were at war from 1689 to 1697; from 1702 to 1713; and from 1743 to 1748. The men in New York or Boston in 1750, who could remember the past sixty years, could thus look back over at least four-and-twenty years of open war; and even in the intervals of professed peace there was a good deal of disturbance on the frontiers. A most frightful sort of warfare it was, ghastly with torture of prisoners and the ruthless murder of women and children. The expense of raising and arming troops for defence was great enough to subject several of the colonies to a heavy burden of debt. In 1750 Massachusetts was just throwing off the load of debt under which she had staggered since 1693; and most of this debt was incurred for expeditions against the French and Algonquins.

[Sidenote: Difficulty of getting the English colonies to act in concert.]

Under these circumstances it was natural that the colonial governments should find it hard to raise enough money for war expenses, and that the governors should think the legislatures too slow in acting. They were slow; for, as is apt to be the case when money is to be borrowed without the best security, there were a good many things to be considered. All this was made worse by the fact that there were so many separate governments, so that each one was inclined to hold back and wait for the others. On the other hand, the French viceroy in Canada had despotic power; the colony which he governed never pretended to be self-supporting; and so, if he could not squeeze money enough out of the people in Canada, he just sent to France for it and got it; for the government of Louis XV. regarded Canada as one of the brightest jewels in its crown, and was always ready to spend money for damaging the English. Accordingly the Frenchman could plan his campaign, call his red men together, and set the whole frontier in a blaze, while the legislatures in Boston or New York were talking about what had better be done in case of invasion. No wonder the royal governors fretted and fumed, and sent home to England dismal accounts of the perverseness of these Americans! Many people in England thought that the colonies were allowed to govern themselves altogether too much, and that for their own good the British government ought to tax them. Once while Sir Robert Walpole was prime minister (1721-1742) some one is said to have advised him to lay a direct tax upon the Americans; but that wise old statesman shook his head. It was bad enough, he said, to be scolded and abused by half the people in the old country; he did not wish to make enemies of every man, woman, and child in the new.

[Sidenote: Need of a union between the English colonies.]

But if the power to raise American armies for the common defence, and to collect money in America for this purpose, was not to be assumed by the British government, was there any way in which unity and promptness of action in time of war could be secured? There was another way, if people could be persuaded to adopt it. The thirteen colonies might be joined together in a federal union; and the federal government, without interfering in the local affairs of any single colony, might be clothed with the power of levying taxes all over the country for purposes of common defence. The royal governors were inclined to favour a union of the colonies, no matter how it might be brought about. They thought it necessary that some decisive step should be taken quickly, for it was evident that the peace of 1748 was only an armed truce. Evidently a great and decisive struggle was at hand. In 1750 the Ohio Company, formed for the purpose of colonizing the valley drained by that river, had surveyed the country as far as the present site of Louisville. In 1753 the French, taking the alarm, crossed Lake Erie, and began to fortify themselves at Presque Isle, and at Venango on the Alleghany river. They seized persons trading within the limits of the Ohio Company, which lay within the territory of Virginia; and accordingly Governor Dinwiddie, of Virginia, selected George Washington--a venturous and hardy young land-surveyor, only twenty-one years old, but gifted with a sagacity beyond his years--and sent him to Venango to warn off the trespassers. It was an exceedingly delicate and dangerous mission, and Washington showed rare skill and courage in this first act of his public career, but the French commander made polite excuses and remained. Next spring the French and English tried each to forestall the other in fortifying the all-important place where the Alleghany and Monongahela rivers unite to form the Ohio, the place long afterward commonly known as the "Gateway of the West," the place where the city of Pittsburgh now stands. In the course of these preliminary manoeuvres Washington was besieged in Fort Necessity by overwhelming numbers, and on July 4, 1754, was obliged to surrender the whole of his force, but obtained leave to march away. So the French got possession of the much-coveted situation, and erected there Fort Duquesne as a menace to all future English intruders. As yet war had not been declared between France and England, but these skirmishings indicated that war in earnest was not far off.

[Sidenote: The Congress at Albany, 1754.]

In view of the approaching war a meeting was arranged at Albany between the principal chiefs of the Six Nations and commissioners from several of the colonies, that the alliance between English and Iroquois might be freshly cemented; and some of the royal governors improved the occasion to call for a Congress of all the colonies, in order to prepare some plan of confederation such as all the colonies might be willing to adopt. At the time of Washington's surrender such a Congress was in session at Albany, but Maryland was the most southerly colony represented in it. The people nowhere showed any interest in it. No public meetings were held in its favour. The only newspaper which warmly approved it was the "Pennsylvania Gazette," which appeared with a union device, a snake divided into thirteen segments, with the motto "Unite or Die!"

The editor of this paper was Benjamin Franklin, then eight-and-forty years of age and already one of the most famous men in America. In the preceding year he had been appointed by the crown postmaster-general for the American colonies, and he had received from the Royal Society the Copley medal for his brilliant discovery that lightning is a discharge of electricity. Franklin was very anxious to see the colonies united in a federal body, and he was now a delegate to the Congress. He drew up a plan of union which the Congress adopted, after a very long debate; and it has ever since been known as the Albany Plan. The federal government was to consist, *first*, of a President or Governor-general, appointed and paid by the crown, and holding office during its pleasure; and *secondly*, of a Grand Council composed of representatives elected every third year by the legislatures of the several colonies. This federal government was not to meddle with the internal affairs of any colony, but on questions of war and such other questions as concerned all the colonies alike, it was to be supreme; and to this end it was to have the power of levying taxes for federal purposes directly upon the people of the several colonies. Philadelphia, as the most centrally situated of the larger towns, was mentioned as a proper seat for the federal government.

The end of our story will show the wonderful foresightedness of Franklin's scheme. If the Revolution had never occurred, we might very likely have sooner or later come to live under a constitution resembling the Albany Plan. On the other hand, if the Albany Plan had been put into operation, it might perhaps have so adjusted the relations of the colonies to the British government that the Revolution would not have occurred. Perhaps, however, it would only have reproduced, on a larger scale, the irrepressible conflict between royal governor and popular assembly. The scheme failed for want of support. The Congress recommended it to the colonial legislatures, but not one of them voted to adopt it. The difficulty was the same in 1754 that it was thirty years later,--only much stronger. The people of one colony saw but little of the people in another, had but few dealings with them, and cared not much about them. They knew and trusted their own local assemblies which sat and voted almost under their eyes; they were not inclined to grant strange powers of taxation to a new assembly distant by a week's journey. This was a point to which people could never have been brought except as the alternative to something confessedly worse.

The failure of the Albany Plan left the question of providing for military defence just where it was before, and the great Seven Years' War came on while governors and assemblies were wrangling to no purpose. In 1755 Braddock's army was unable to get support except from the steadfast personal exertions of Franklin, who used his great influence with the farmers of Pennsylvania to obtain horses, wagons, and provisions, pledging his own property for their payment. Nevertheless, as the war went on and the people of the colonies became fully alive to its importance, they did contribute liberally both in men and in money, and at last it appeared that in proportion to their wealth and population they had done even more than the regular army and the royal exchequer toward overthrowing the common enemy.

When the war came to an end in 1763 the whole face of things in America was changed. Seldom, if ever, had the world seen so complete a victory. France no longer possessed so much as an acre of ground in all North America. The unknown regions beyond the Mississippi river were handed over to Spain in payment for bootless assistance rendered to France toward the close of the war. Spain also received New Orleans, while Florida, which then reached westward nearly to New Orleans, passed from Spanish into British hands. The whole country north of Florida and east of the Mississippi river, including Canada, was now English. A strong combination of Indian tribes, chiefly Algonquin, under the lead of the Ottawa sachem Pontiac, made a last desperate attempt, after the loss of their French allies, to cripple the English; but by 1765, after many harrowing scenes of bloodshed, these red men were crushed. There was no power left that could threaten the peace of the thirteen colonies unless it were the mother-country herself. "Well," said the French minister, the Duke de Choiseul, as he signed the treaty that shut France out of North America, "so we are gone; it will be England's turn next!" And like a prudent seeker after knowledge, as he was, the Duke presently bethought him of an able and high-minded man, the Baron de Kalb, and sent him in 1767 to America, to look about and see if there were not good grounds for his bold prophecy.

CHAPTER IV. THE STAMP ACT, AND THE REVENUE LAWS.

It did not take four years after the peace of 1763 to show how rapidly the new situation of affairs was bearing fruit in America. The war had taught its lessons. Earlier wars had menaced portions of the frontier, and had been fought by single colonies or alliances of two or three. This war had menaced the whole frontier, and the colonies, acting for the first time in general concert, had acquired some dim notion of their united strength. Soldiers and officers by and by to be arrayed against one another had here fought as allies,--John Stark and Israel Putnam by the side of William Howe; Horatio Gates by the side of Thomas Gage,--and it had not always been the regulars that bore off the palm for skill and endurance. One young man, of immense energy and fiery temper, united to rare prudence and fertility of resource, had already become famous enough to be talked about in England; in George Washington the Virginians recognized a tower of strength.

[Sidenote: Consequences of the great French War.]

[Sidenote: Need for a steady revenue.]

The overthrow of their ancient enemy, while further increasing the self-confidence of the Americans, at the same time removed the principal check which had hitherto kept their differences with the British government from coming to an open rupture. Formerly the dread of French attack had tended to make the Americans complaisant toward the king's ministers, while at time it made the king's ministers unwilling to lose the good will of the Americans. Now that the check was removed, the continuance or revival of the old disputes at once foreboded trouble; and the old occasions for dispute were far from having ceased. On the contrary the war itself had given them fresh vitality. If money had been needed before, it was still more needed now. The war had entailed a heavy burden of expense upon the British government as well as upon the colonies. The national debt of Great Britain was much increased, and there were many who thought that, since the Americans shared in the benefits of the war they ought also to share in the burden which it left behind it. People in England who used this argument did not realize that the

Americans had really contributed as much as could reasonably be expected to the support of the war, and that it had left behind it debts to be paid in America as well as in England. But there was another argument which made it seem reasonable to many Englishmen that the colonists should be taxed. It seemed right that a small military force should be kept up in America, for defence of the frontiers against the Indians, even if there were no other enemies to be dreaded. The events of Pontiac's war now showed that there was clearly need of such a force; and the experience of the royal governors for half a century had shown that it was very difficult to get the colonial legislatures to vote money for any such purpose. Hence there grew up in England a feeling that taxes ought to be raised in America as a contribution to the war debt and to the military defence of the colonies; and in order that such taxes should be fairly distributed and promptly collected, it was felt that the whole business ought to be placed under the direct supervision and control of parliament. In accordance with this feeling the new prime minister, George Grenville in 1764 announced his intention of passing a Stamp Act for the easier collection of revenue in America. Meanwhile things had happened in America which had greatly irritated the people, especially in Boston, so that they were in the mood for resisting anything that looked like encroachment on the part of the British government. To understand this other source of irritation, we must devote a few words to the laws by which that government had for a long time undertaken to regulate the commerce of the American colonies.

[Sidenote: What European colonies were supposed to be founded for.]

When European nations began to plant colonies in America, they treated them in accordance with a theory which prevailed until it was upset by the American Revolution. According to this ignorant and barbarous theory, a colony was a community which existed only for the purpose of enriching the country which had founded it. At the outset, the Spanish notion of a colony was that of a military station, which might plunder the heathen for the benefit of the hungry treasury of the Most Catholic monarch. But this theory was short-lived, like the enjoyment of the plunder which it succeeded in extorting. According to the principles and practice of France and England--and of Spain also, after the first romantic fury of buccaneering had spent itself--the great object in founding a colony, besides increasing one's general importance in the world and the area of one's dominions on the map, was to create a dependent community for the purpose of trading with it. People's ideas about trade were very absurd. It was not understood that when two parties trade with each other freely, both must be gainers, or else one would soon stop trading. It was supposed that in trade, just as in gambling or betting, what the one party gains the other loses. Accordingly laws were made to regulate trade so that, as far as possible, all the loss might fall upon the colonies and all the gain accrue to the mother-country. In order to attain this object, the colonies were required to confine their trade entirely to England. No American colony could send its tobacco or its rice or its indigo to France or to Holland, or to any other country than England; nor could it buy a yard of French silk or a pound of Chinese tea except from English merchants. In this way English merchants sought to secure for themselves a monopoly of purchases and a monopoly of sales. By a further provision, although American ships might take goods to England, the carrying-trade between the different colonies was strictly confined to British ships. Next, in order to protect British manufacturers from competition, it was thought necessary to prohibit the colonists from manufacturing. They might grow wool, but it must be carried to England to be woven into cloth; they might smelt iron, but it must be carried to England to be made into ploughshares. Finally, in order to protect British farmers and their landlords, corn-laws were enacted, putting a prohibitory tariff on all kinds of grain and other farm produce shipped from the colonies to ports in Great Britain.

Such absurd and tyrannical laws had begun to be made in the reign of Charles II., and by 1750 not less than twenty-nine acts of parliament had been passed in this spirit. If these laws had been strictly enforced, the American Revolution would probably have come sooner than it did. In point of fact they were seldom strictly enforced, because so long as the French were a power in America the British government felt that it could not afford to irritate the colonists. In spite of laws to the contrary, the carrying-trade between the different colonies was almost monopolized by vessels owned, built, and manned in New England; and the smuggling of foreign goods into Boston and New York and other seaport towns was winked at.

[Sidenote: Writs of assistance.]

It was in 1761, immediately after the overthrow of the French in Canada, that attempts were made to enforce the revenue laws more strictly than heretofore; and trouble was at once threatened. Charles Paxton, the principal officer of the custom-house in Boston, applied to the Superior Court to grant him the authority to use "writs of assistance" in searching for smuggled goods. A writ of assistance was a general search-warrant, empowering the officer armed with it to enter, by force if necessary, any dwelling-house or warehouse where contraband goods were supposed to be stored or hidden. A special search-warrant was one in which the name of the suspected person, and the house which it was proposed to search, were accurately specified, and the goods which it was intended to seize were as far as possible described. In the use of such special warrants there was not much danger of gross injustice or oppression, because the court would not be likely to grant one unless strong evidence could be brought against the person whom it named. But the general search-warrant, or "writ of assistance," as it was called because men try to cover up the ugliness of hateful things by giving them innocent names, was quite a different affair. It was a blank form upon which the custom-house officer might fill in the names of persons and descriptions of houses and goods to suit himself. Then he could go and break into the houses and seize the goods, and if need be summon the sheriff and his *posse* to help him in overcoming and browbeating the owner. The writ of assistance was therefore an abominable instrument of tyranny. Such writs had been allowed by a statute of the evil reign of Charles II.; a statute of William III. had clothed custom-house officers in the colonies with like powers to those which they possessed in England; and neither of these statutes had been repealed. There can therefore be little doubt that the issue of such search-warrants was strictly legal, unless the authority of Parliament to make laws for the colonies was to be denied.

[Sidenote: James Otis.]

James Otis then held the crown office of advocate-general, with an ample salary and prospects of high favour from government. When the revenue officers called upon him, in view of his position, to defend their cause, he resigned his office and at once undertook to act as counsel for the merchants of Boston in their protest against the issue of the writs. A large fee was offered him, but he refused it. "In such a cause," said he, "I despise all fees." The case was tried in the council-chamber at the east end of the old town-hall, or what is now known as the "Old State-House," in Boston. Chief-justice Hutchinson presided, and Jeremiah Gridley, one of the greatest lawyers of that day, argued the case for the writs in a very powerful speech. The reply of Otis, which took five hours in the delivery, was one of the greatest speeches of modern times. It went beyond the particular legal question at issue, and took up the whole question of the constitutional relations between the colonies and the mother-country. At the bottom of this, as of all the disputes that led to the Revolution, lay the ultimate question whether Americans were bound to yield obedience to laws which they had no share in making. This question, and the spirit that answered it flatly and doggedly in the negative, were heard like an undertone pervading all the arguments in Otis's wonderful speech, and it was because of this that the young lawyer John Adams, who was present, afterward declared that on that day "the child Independence was born." Chief-justice Hutchinson was a man of great ability and as sincere a patriot as any American of his time. He could feel the force of Otis's argument, but he believed that Parliament was the supreme legislative body for the whole British empire, and furthermore that it was the duty of a judge to follow the law as it existed. He reserved his decision until advice could be had from the law-officers of the crown in London; and when next term he was instructed by them to grant the writs, this result added fresh impetus to the spirit that Otis's eloquence had aroused. The custom-house officers, armed with their writs, began breaking into warehouses and seizing goods which were said to have been smuggled. In this rough way they confiscated private property to the value of many thousands of pounds; but sometimes the owners of warehouses armed themselves and barricaded their doors and windows, and thus the officers were often successfully defied, for the sheriff was far from prompt in coming to aid them.

[Sidenote: Patrick Henry, and the Parsons' Cause.]

While such things were going on in Boston, the people of Virginia were wrought into fierce excitement by what was known as the "Parsons' Cause." The Church of England was at that time established by law in Virginia, and its clergymen, appointed by English bishops, were unpopular. In 1758 the legislature, under the pressure of the French war, had passed an act which affected all public dues and incidentally diminished the salaries of the clergy. Complaints were made to the Bishop of London, and the act of 1758 was vetoed by the king in council. Several clergymen then brought suits to recover the unpaid portions of their salaries. In the first test case there could be no doubt that the royal veto was legal enough, and the court therefore decided in favour of the plaintiff. But it now remained to settle before a jury the amount of the damages. It was on this occasion, in December, 1763, that the great orator Patrick Henry made his first speech in the court-room and at once became famous. He declared that no power on earth could take away from Virginia the right to make laws for herself, and that in annulling a wholesome law at the request of a favoured class in the community "a king, from being the father of his people, degenerates into a tyrant, and forfeits all right to obedience." This bold talk aroused much excitement and some uproar, but the jury instantly responded by assessing the parson's damages at one penny, and in 1765 Henry was elected a member of the colonial assembly.

Thus almost at the same time in Massachusetts and in Virginia the preliminary scenes of the Revolution occurred in the court-room. In each case the representatives of the crown had the letter of the law on their side, but the principles of the only sound public policy, by which a Revolution could be avoided, were those that were defended by the advocates of the people. At each successive move on the part of the British government which looked like an encroachment upon the rights of Americans, the sympathy between these two leading colonies now grew stronger and stronger.

It was in 1763 that George Grenville became prime minister, a man of whom Macaulay says that he knew of "no national interests except those which are expressed by pounds, shillings, and pence." Grenville proceeded to introduce into Parliament two measures which had consequences of which, he little dreamed. The first of these measures was the Molasses Act, the second was the Stamp Act.

[Sidenote: The Molasses Act.]

Properly speaking, the Molasses Act was an old law which Grenville now made up his mind to revive and enforce. The commercial wealth of the New England colonies depended largely upon their trade with the fish which their fishermen caught along the coast and as far out as the banks of Newfoundland. The finest fish could be sold in Europe, but the poorer sort found their chief market in the French West Indies. The French government, in order to ensure a market for the molasses raised in these islands, would not allow the planters to give anything else in exchange for fish. Great quantities of molasses were therefore carried to New England, and what was not needed there for domestic use was distilled into rum, part of which was consumed at home, and the rest carried chiefly to Africa wherewith to buy slaves to be sold to the southern colonies. All this trade required many ships, and thus kept up a lively demand for New England lumber, besides finding employment for thousands of sailors and shipwrights. Now in 1733 the British government took it into its head to "protect" its sugar planters in the English West Indies by compelling the New England merchants to buy all their molasses from them; and with this end in view it forthwith laid upon all sugar and molasses imported into North America from the French islands a duty so heavy that, if it had been enforced, it would have stopped all such importation. It is very doubtful if this measure would have attained the end which the British government had in view. Probably it would not have made much difference in the export of molasses from the English West Indies to New England, because the islanders happened not to want the fish which their French neighbours coveted. But the New Englanders could see that the immediate result would be to close the market for their cheaper kinds of fish, and thus ruin their trade in lumber and rum, besides shutting up many a busy shipyard and turning more than 5000 sailors out of employment. It was estimated that the yearly loss to New England would exceed £300,000. It was hardly wise in Great Britain to entail such a loss upon some of her best customers; for with their incomes thus cut down, it was not to be expected that the people of New England would be able to buy as many farming tools, dishes, and pieces of furniture, garments of silk or wool, and wines or other luxuries, from British merchants as before. The government in passing its act of 1733 did not think of these consequences; but it proved to be impossible to enforce the act without causing more disturbance than the government felt prepared to encounter. Now in 1764 Grenville announced that the act was to be enforced, and of course the machinery of writs of assistance was to be employed for that purpose. Henceforth all molasses from the French islands must either pay the prohibitory duty or be seized without ceremony.

Loud and fierce was the indignation of New England over this revival of the Molasses Act. Even without the Stamp Act, it might very likely have led that part of the country to make armed resistance, but in such case it is not so sure that the southern and middle colonies would have come to the aid of New England. But in the Stamp Act Grenville provided the colonies with an issue which concerned one as much as another, and upon which they were accordingly sure to unite in resistance. It was also a much better issue for the Americans to take up, for it was not a mere revival of an old act; it was a new departure; it was an imposition of a kind to which the Americans had never before been called upon to submit, and in resisting it they were sure to enlist the sympathies of a good many powerful people in England.

[Sidenote: The Stamp Act.]

The Stamp Act was a direct tax laid upon the whole American people by Parliament, a legislative body in which they were not represented. The British government had no tyrannical purpose in devising this tax. A stamp duty had already been suggested in 1755 by William Shirley, royal governor of Massachusetts, a worthy man and much more of a favourite with the people than most of his class. Shirley recommended it as the least disagreeable kind of tax, and the easiest to collect. It did not call for any hateful searching of people's houses and shops, or any unpleasant questions about their incomes, or about their invested or hoarded wealth. It only required that legal documents and commercial instruments should be written, and newspapers printed, on stamped paper. Of all kinds of direct tax none can be less annoying, except for one reason; it is exceedingly difficult to evade such a tax; it enforces itself. For these reasons Grenville decided to adopt it. He arranged it so that all the officers charged with the business of selling the stamped paper should be Americans; and he gave formal notice of the measure in March, 1764, a year beforehand, in order to give the colonies time to express their opinions about it.

[Sidenote: Samuel Adams.]

In the Boston town-meeting in May, almost as soon as the news had arrived, the American view of the case was very clearly set forth in a series of resolutions drawn up by Samuel Adams. This was the first of the remarkable state papers from the pen of that great man, who now, at the age of forty-two, was just entering upon a glorious career. Samuel Adams was a graduate of Harvard College in the class of 1740. He had been reared in politics from boyhood, for his father, a deacon of the Old South Church, had been chief spokesman of the popular party in its disputes with the royal governors. Of all the agencies in organizing resistance to Great Britain none were more powerful than the New England town-meetings, among which that of the people of Boston stood preëminent, and in the Boston town-meeting for more than thirty years no other man exerted so much influence as Samuel Adams. This was because of his keen intelligence and persuasive talk, his spotless integrity, indomitable courage, unselfish and unwearying devotion to the public good, and broad sympathy with all classes of people. He was a thorough democrat. He respected the dignity of true manhood wherever he found it, and could talk with sailors and shipwrights like one of themselves, while at the same time in learned argument he had few superiors. He has been called the "Father of the Revolution," and was no doubt its most conspicuous figure before 1775, as Washington certainly was after that date.

This earliest state paper of Samuel Adams contained the first formal and public denial of the right of Parliament to tax the colonies, because it was not a body in which their people were represented. The resolutions were adopted by the Massachusetts assembly, and a similar action was taken by Connecticut, New York, Pennsylvania, Virginia, and South Carolina. The colonies professed their willingness to raise money in answer to requisitions upon their assemblies, which were the only bodies competent to lay taxes in America. Memorials stating these views were sent to England, and the colony of Pennsylvania sent Dr. Franklin to represent its case at the British court. Franklin remained in London until the spring of 1775 as agent first for Pennsylvania, afterward for Massachusetts, New Jersey, and Georgia,--a kind of diplomatic representative of the views and claims of the Americans.

[Sidenote: The Virginia Resolutions, 1765.]

Grenville told Franklin that he wished to do things as pleasantly as possible, and was not disposed to insist upon the Stamp Act, if the Americans could suggest anything better. But when it appeared that no alternative was offered except to fall back upon the old clumsy system of requisitions, Grenville naturally replied that there ought to be some more efficient method of raising money for the defence of the frontier. Accordingly in March, 1765, the Stamp Act was passed, with so little debate that people hardly noticed what was going on. But when the news reached America there was an outburst of wrath that was soon heard and felt in London. In May the Virginia legislature was assembled. George Washington was sitting there in his seat, and Thomas Jefferson, then a law-student, was listening eagerly from outside the door, when Patrick Henry introduced the famous resolutions in which he declared, among other things, that an attempt to vest the power of taxation in any other body than the colonial assembly was a menace to the common freedom of Englishmen, whether in Britain or in America, and that the people of Virginia were not bound to obey any law enacted in disregard of this principle. The language of the resolutions was bold enough, but a keener edge was put upon it by the defiant note which rang out from Henry in the course of the debate, when he commended the example of Tarquin and Cæsar and Charles I. to the attention of George III. "If this be treason," he exclaimed, as the speaker tried to call him to order, "if this be treason, make the most of it!"

The other colonies were not slow in acting. Massachusetts called for a general congress, in order that all might discuss the situation and agree upon some course to be pursued in common. South Carolina responded most cordially, at the instance of her noble, learned, and far-sighted patriot, Christopher Gadsden. On the 7th of October, delegates from nine colonies met in a congress at New York, adopted resolutions like those of Virginia, and sent a memorial to the king, whose sovereignty over them they admitted, and a remonstrance to Parliament, whose authority to tax them they denied. The meeting of this congress was in itself a prophecy of what was to happen if the British government should persist in the course upon which it had now entered.

[Sidenote: Stamp Act riots.]

Meanwhile the summer had witnessed riots in many places, and one of these was extremely disgraceful. Chief-justice Hutchinson had tried to dissuade the ministry from passing the Stamp Act, but an impression had got abroad among the wharves and waterside taverns of Boston that he had not only favoured it but had gone out of his way to send information to London, naming certain merchants as smugglers. Under the influence of this mistaken notion, on the night of the 26th of August a drunken mob plundered Hutchinson's house in Boston and destroyed his library, which was probably the finest in America at that time. Here, as is apt to be the case, the mob selected the wrong victim. Its shameful act was denounced by the people of Massachusetts, and the chief-justice was indemnified by the legislature. In the other instances the riots were of an innocent sort. Stamp officers were forced to resign. Boxes of stamped paper arriving by ship were burned or thrown into the sea, and at length the governor of New York was compelled by a mob to surrender all the stamps entrusted to his care. These things were done for the most part under the direction of societies of workingmen known as "Sons of Liberty," who were pledged to resist the execution of the Stamp Act. At the same time associations of merchants declared that they would buy no more goods from England until the act should be repealed, and lawyers entered into agreements not to treat any document as invalidated by the absence of the required stamp. As for the editors, they published their newspapers decorated with a grinning skull and cross-bones instead of the stamp.

[Sidenote: Repeal of the Stamp Act.]

These demonstrations produced their effect in England. In July, 1765, the Grenville ministry fell, and the new government, with Lord Rockingham at its head, was more inclined to pay heed to the wishes and views of the Americans. The debate over the repeal of the Stamp Act lasted nearly three months and was one of the fiercest that had been heard in Parliament for many a day. William Pitt declared that he rejoiced in the resistance of the Americans, and urged that the act should be repealed because Parliament ought never to have passed it; but there were very few who took this view. As the result of the long debate, at the end of March, 1766, the Stamp Act was repealed, and a Declaratory Act was passed in which Parliament said in effect that it had a right to make such laws for the Americans if it chose to do so.

The people of London, as well as the Americans, hailed with delight the repeal of the Stamp Act; but the real trouble had now only begun. The resolutions of Samuel Adams and Patrick Henry and their approval by the Congress at New York had thrown the question of American taxation into the whirlpool of British politics, and there it was to stay until it worked a change for the better in England as well as in America.

[Sidenote: How the question was affected by British politics.]

The principle that people must not be taxed except by their representatives had been to some extent recognized in England for five hundred years, and it was really the fundamental principle of English liberty, but it was only very imperfectly that it had been put into practice. In the eighteenth century the House of Commons was very far from being a body that fairly represented the people of Great Britain. For a long time there had been no change in the distribution of seats, and meanwhile the population had been increasing very differently in different parts of the kingdom. Thus great cities which had grown up in recent times, such as Sheffield and Manchester, had no representatives in Parliament, while many little boroughs with a handful of inhabitants had their representatives. Some such boroughs had been granted representation by Henry VIII. in order to create a majority for his measures in the House of Commons. Others were simply petty towns that had dwindled away, somewhat as the mountain villages of New England have dwindled since the introduction of railroads. The famous Old Sarum had members in Parliament long after it had ceased to have any inhabitants. Seats for these rotten boroughs, as they were called, were simply bought and sold. Political life in England was exceedingly corrupt;

some of the best statesmen indulged in wholesale bribery as if it were the most innocent thing in the world. The country was really governed by a few great families, some of whose members sat in the House of Lords and others in the House of Commons. Their measures were often noble and patriotic in the highest degree, but when bribery and corruption seemed necessary for carrying them, such means were employed without scruple.

[Sidenote: George III. and his political schemes.]

When George III. came to the throne in 1760, the great families which had thus governed England for half a century belonged to the party known as Old Whigs. Under their rule the power of the crown had been reduced to insignificance, and the modern system of cabinet government by a responsible ministry had begun to grow up. The Tory families during this period had been very unpopular, because of their sympathy with the Stuart pretenders who had twice attempted to seize the crown and given the country a brief taste of civil war. By 1760 the Tories saw that the cause of the Stuarts was hopeless, and so they were inclined to transfer their affections to the new king. George III. was a young man of narrow intelligence and poor education, but he entertained very strong opinions as to the importance of his kingly office. He meant to make himself a real king, like the king of France or the king of Spain. He was determined to break down the power of the Old Whigs and the system of cabinet government, and as the Old Whigs had been growing unpopular, it seemed quite possible, with the aid of the Tories, to accomplish this. George was quite decorous in behaviour, and, although subject to fits of insanity which became more troublesome in his later years, he had a fairly good head for business. Industrious as a beaver and obstinate as a mule, he was an adept in political trickery. In the corrupt use of patronage he showed himself able to beat the Old Whigs at their own game, and with the aid of the Tories he might well believe himself capable of reviving for his own benefit the lost power of the crown.

[Sidenote: The "New Whigs" and parliamentary reform.]

Beside these two parties a third had been for some time growing up which was in some essential points opposed to both of them. This third party was that of the New Whigs. They wished to reform the representation in Parliament in such wise as to disfranchise the rotten boroughs and give representatives to great towns like Leeds and Manchester. They held that it was contrary to the principles of English liberty that the inhabitants of such great towns should be obliged to pay taxes in pursuance of laws which they had no share in making. The leader of the New Whigs was the greatest Englishman of the eighteenth century, the elder William Pitt, now about to pass into the House of Lords as Earl of Chatham. Their leader next in importance, William Petty, Earl of Shelburne, was in 1765 a young man of eight-and-twenty, and afterward came to be known as one of the most learned and sagacious statesmen of his time. These men were the forerunners of the great liberal leaders of the nineteenth century, such men as Russell and Cobden and Gladstone. Their first decisive and overwhelming victory was the passage of Lord John Russell's Reform Bill in 1832, but the agitation for reform was begun by William Pitt in 1745, and his famous son came very near winning the victory on that question in 1782.

Now this question of parliamentary reform was intimately related to the question of taxing the American colonies. From some points of view they might be considered one and the same question. At a meeting of Presbyterian ministers in Philadelphia, it was pertinently asked, "Have two men chosen to represent a poor English borough that has sold its votes to the highest bidder any pretence to say that they represent Virginia or Pennsylvania? And have four hundred such fellows a right to take our liberties?" In Parliament, on the other hand, as well as at London dinner tables, and in newspapers and pamphlets, it was repeatedly urged that the Americans need not make so much fuss about being taxed without being represented, for in that respect they were no worse off than the people of Sheffield or Birmingham. To this James Otis replied, "Don't talk to us any more about those towns, for we are tired of such a flimsy argument. If they are not represented, they ought to be;" and by the New Whigs this retort was greeted with applause.

The opinions and aims of the three different parties were reflected in the long debate over the repeal of the Stamp Act. The Tories wanted to have the act continued and enforced, and such was the wish of the king. Both sections of Whigs were in favour of repeal, but for very different reasons. Pitt and the New Whigs, being advocates of parliamentary reform, came out flatly in support of the principle that there should be no taxation without representation. Edmund Burke and the Old Whigs, being opposed to parliamentary reform and in favour of keeping things just as they were, could not adopt such an argument; and accordingly they based their condemnation of the Stamp Act upon grounds of pure expediency. They argued that it was not worth while, for the sake of a little increase of revenue, to irritate three million people and run the risk of getting drawn into a situation from which there would be no escape except in either retreating or fighting. There was much practical wisdom in this Old Whig argument, and it was the one which prevailed when Parliament repealed the Stamp Act and expressly stated that it did so only on grounds of expediency.

[Sidenote: Why George III. was ready to pick a quarrel with the Americans.]

There was one person, however, who was far from satisfied with this result, and that was George III. He was opposed to parliamentary reform for much the same reason that the Old Whigs were opposed to it, because he felt that it threatened him with political ruin. The Old Whigs needed the rotten boroughs in order to maintain their own control over Parliament and the country. The king needed them because he felt himself able to wrest them from the Old Whigs by intrigue and corruption, and thus hoped to build up his own power. He believed, with good reason, that the suppression of the rotten boroughs and the granting of fair and equal representation would soon put a stronger curb upon the crown than ever. Accordingly there were no men whom he dreaded and wished to put down so much as the New Whigs; and he felt that in the repeal of the Stamp Act, no matter on what ground, they had come altogether too near winning a victory. He felt that this outrageous doctrine that people must not be taxed except by their representatives needed to be sternly rebuked, and thus he found himself in the right sort of temper for picking a fresh quarrel with the Americans.

[Sidenote: Charles Townshend and his revenue acts, 1767.]

[Sidenote: Lord North.]

An occasion soon presented itself. One of the king's devices for breaking down the system of cabinet government was to select his ministers from different parties, so that they might be unable to work harmoniously together. Owing to the peculiar divisions of parties in Parliament he was for some years able to carry out this policy, and while his cabinets were thus weak and divided, he was able to use his control of patronage with telling effect. In July, 1766, he got rid of Lord Rockingham and his Old Whigs, and formed a new ministry made up from all parties. It contained Pitt, who had now, as Earl of Chatham, gone into the House of Lords, and at the same time Charles Townshend, as Chancellor of the Exchequer. Townshend, a brilliant young man, without any political principles worth mentioning, was the most conspicuous among a group of wire-pullers who were coming to be known as "the king's friends." Serious illness soon kept Chatham at home, and left Townshend all-powerful in the cabinet, because he was bold and utterly unscrupulous and had the king to back him. His audacity knew no limits, and he made up his mind that the time had come for gathering all the disputed American questions, as far as possible, into one bundle, and disposing of them once for all. So in May, 1767, he brought forward in Parliament a series of acts for raising and applying a revenue in America. The colonists, he said, had objected to a direct tax, but they had often submitted to port duties, and could not reasonably refuse to do so again. Duties were accordingly to be laid on glass, paper, lead, and painter's colours; on wine, oil, and fruits, if carried directly to America from Spain and Portugal; and especially on tea. A board of commissioners was to be established at Boston, to superintend the collection of revenue throughout the colonies, and writs of assistance were to be expressly legalized. The salaries of these commissioners were to be paid out of the revenue thus collected. Governors, judges, and crown-attorneys were to be made independent of the colonial legislatures by having their salaries paid by the crown out of this same fund. A small army was also to be kept up; and if after providing for these various expenses, any surplus remained, it could be used by the crown in giving pensions to Americans and thus be made to serve as a corruption-fund. These measures were adopted on the 29th of June, and as if to refute anybody who might be inclined to think that rashness could no further go, Townshend accompanied them with a special act directed against the New York legislature, which had refused to obey an order concerning the quartering of troops. By way of punishment, Townshend now suspended the legislature. A few weeks after carrying these measures Townshend died of a fever, and his place was taken by Lord North, eldest son of the Earl of Guilford. North was thirty-five years of age. He was amiable and witty, and an excellent debater, but without force of will. He let the king rule him, and was at the same time able to show a strong hand in the House of Commons, so that the king soon came to regard him as a real treasure. Soon after North's appointment, Lord Chatham and other friends of America in the cabinet resigned their places and were succeeded by friends of the king. From 1768 to 1782 George III. was to all intents and purposes his own prime minister, and contrived to keep a majority in Parliament. During those fourteen years the American question was uppermost, and his policy was at all hazards to force the colonists to abandon their position that taxation must go hand in hand with representation.

[Sidenote: What the Townshend acts really meant.]

This purpose was already apparent in Charles Townshend's acts. They were not at all like previous acts imposing port duties to which the Americans had submitted. British historians sometimes speak of the American Revolution as an affair which grew out of a mere dispute about money; and even among Americans, in ordinary conversation and sometimes in current literature, the unwillingness of our forefathers to pay a tax of threepence a pound on tea is mentioned without due reference to the attendant circumstances which made them refuse to pay such a tax. We cannot hope to understand the fierce wrath by which they were animated unless we bear in mind not only the simple fact of the tax, but also the spirit in which it was levied and the purpose for which the revenue was to be used. The Molasses Act threatening the ruin of New England commerce was still on the statute-book, and commissioners, armed with odious search-warrants for enforcing this and other tyrannical laws, were on their way to America. For more than half a century the people had jealously guarded against the abuse of power by the royal governors by making them dependent upon the legislatures for their salaries. Now they were all at once to be made independent, so that they might even dismiss the legislatures, and if need be call for troops to help them. The judges, moreover, with their power over men's lives and property, were no longer to be responsible to the people. If these changes were to be effected, it would be nothing less than a revolution by which the Americans would be deprived of their liberty. And, to crown all, the money by which this revolution was to be brought about was to be contributed in the shape of port duties by the Americans themselves! To expect our forefathers to submit to such legislation as this was about as sensible as it would have been to expect them to obey an order to buy halters and hang themselves.

When the news of the Townshend acts reached Massachusetts, the assembly at its next session took a decided stand. Besides a petition to the king and letters to several leading British statesmen, it issued a circular letter addressed to the other twelve colonies, asking for their friendly advice and coöperation with reference to the Townshend measures. These papers were written by Samuel Adams. The circular letter was really an invitation to the other colonies to concert measures of resistance if it should be found necessary. It enraged the king, and presently an order came across the ocean to Francis Bernard, royal governor of Massachusetts, to demand of the assembly that it rescind its circular letter, under penalty of instant dissolution. Otis exclaimed that Great Britain had better rescind the Townshend acts if she did not wish to lose her colonies. The assembly decided, by a vote of 92 to 17, that it would not rescind. This flat defiance was everywhere applauded. The assemblies of the other colonies were ordered to take no notice of the Massachusetts circular, but the order was generally disobeyed, and in several cases the governors turned the assemblies out of doors. The atmosphere of America now became alive with politics; more meetings were held, more speeches made, and more pamphlets printed, than ever before.

[Sidenote: The quarrel was not between England and America, but between George III. and the principles which the Americans maintained.]

In England the dignified and manly course of the Americans was generally greeted with applause by Whigs of whatever sort, except those who had come into the somewhat widening circle of "the king's friends." The Old Whigs,--Burke, Fox, Conway, Savile, Lord John Cavendish, and the Duke of Richmond; and the New Whigs,--Chatham, Shelburne, Camden, Dunning, Barré, and Beckford; steadily defended the Americans throughout the whole of the Revolutionary crisis, and the weight of the best intelligence in the country was certainly on their side. Could they have acted as a united body, could Burke and Fox have joined forces in harmony with Chatham and Shelburne, they might have thwarted the king and prevented the rupture with America. But George III. profited by the hopeless division between these two Whig parties; and as the quarrel with America grew fiercer, he succeeded in arraying the national pride to some extent upon his side and against the Whigs. This made him feel stronger and stimulated his zeal against the Americans. He felt that if he could first crush Whig principles in America, he could then turn and crush them in England. In this he was correct, except that he miscalculated the strength of the Americans. It was the defeat of his schemes in America that ensured their defeat in England. It is quite wrong and misleading, therefore, to remember the Revolutionary War as a struggle between the British people and the American people. It was a struggle between two hostile principles, each of which was represented in both countries. In winning the good fight, our forefathers won a victory for England as well as for America. What was crushed was George III. and the kind of despotism which he wished to fasten upon America in order that he might fasten it upon England. If the memory of George III. deserves to be execrated, it is especially because he succeeded in giving to his own selfish struggle for power the appearance of a struggle between the people of England and the people of America; and in so doing, he sowed seeds of enmity and distrust between two glorious nations that, for their own sakes and for the welfare of mankind, ought never for one moment to be allowed to forget their brotherhood. Time, however, is rapidly repairing the damage which George III.'s policy wrought, and it need in nowise disturb our narrative. In this brief sketch we must omit hundreds of interesting details; but, if we would look at things from the right point of view, we must bear in mind that every act of George III., from 1768 onward, which brought on and carried on the Revolutionary War, was done in spite of the earnest protest of many of the best people in England; and that the king's wrong-headed policy prevailed only because he was able, through corrupt methods, to command a parliament which did not really represent the people. Had the principles in support of which Lord Chatham joined hands with Samuel Adams for one moment prevailed, the king's schemes would have collapsed like a soap-bubble.

As it was, in 1768 the king succeeded, in spite of strong opposition, in carrying his point. He saw that the American colonies were disposed to resist the Townshend acts, and that in this defiant attitude Massachusetts was the ringleader. The Massachusetts circular pointed toward united action on the part of the colonies. Above all things it was desirable to prevent any such union, and accordingly the king decided to make his principal attack upon Massachusetts, while dealing more kindly with the other colonies. Thus he hoped Massachusetts might be isolated and humbled, and in this belief he proceeded faster and more rashly than if he had supposed himself to be dealing with a united America. In order to catch Samuel Adams and James Otis, and get them sent over to England for trial, he attempted to revive an old statute of Henry VIII. about treason committed abroad; and in order to enforce the revenue laws in spite of all opposition, he ordered troops to be sent to Boston.

[Sidenote: Troops sent to Boston.]

This was a very harsh measure, and some excuse was needed to justify it before Parliament. It was urged that Boston was a disorderly town, and the sacking of Hutchinson's house could be cited in support of this view. Then in June, 1768, there was a slight conflict between townspeople and revenue officers, in which no one was hurt, but which led to a great town-meeting in the Old South Meeting-House, and gave Governor Bernard an opportunity for saying that he was intimidated and hindered in the execution of the laws. The king's real purpose, however, in sending troops was not so much to keep the peace as to enforce the Townshend acts, and so the people of Boston understood it. Except for these odious and tyrannical laws, there was nothing that threatened disturbance in Boston. The arrival of British troops at Long Wharf, in the autumn of 1768, simply increased the danger of disturbance, and in a certain sense it may be said to have been the beginning of the Revolutionary War. Very few people realized this at the time, but Samuel Adams now made up his mind that the only way in which the American colonies could preserve their liberties was to unite in some sort of federation and declare themselves independent of Great Britain. It was with regret that he had come to this conclusion, and he was very slow in proclaiming it, but after 1768 he kept it distinctly before his mind. He saw clearly the end toward which public opinion was gradually drifting, and because of his great influence over the Boston town-meeting and the Massachusetts assembly, this clearness of purpose made him for the next seven years the most formidable of the king's antagonists in America.

The people of Boston were all the more indignant at the arrival of troops in their town because the king in his hurry to send them had even disregarded the act of Parliament which provided for such cases. According to that act the soldiers ought to have been lodged in Castle William on one of the little islands in the harbour. Even according to British-made law they had no business to be quartered in Boston so long as there was room for them, in the Castle. During the next seventeen months the people made several formal protests against their presence in town, and asked for their removal. But these protests were all fruitless until innocent blood had been shed. The soldiers generally behaved no worse than rough troopers on such occasions are apt to do, and the townspeople for the most part preserved decorum, but quarrels now and then occurred, and after a while became frequent. In September, 1769, James Otis was brutally assaulted at the British Coffee House by one of the commissioners of customs aided and abetted by two or three army officers. His health was already feeble and in this affray he was struck on the head with a sword and so badly injured that he afterward became insane. After this the feeling of the people toward the soldiers was more bitter than ever. In February, 1770, there was much disturbance. Toward the end of the month an informer named Richardson fired from his window into a crowd and killed a little boy about eleven years of age, named Christopher Snyder. The funeral of this poor boy, the first victim of the Revolution, was attended on Monday, the 26th, by a great procession of citizens, including those foremost in wealth and influence.

[Sidenote: The "Boston Massacre."]

The rest of that week was full of collisions which on Friday almost amounted to a riot and led the governor's council to consider seriously whether the troops ought not to be removed. But before they had settled the question the crisis came on Monday evening, March 5, in an affray before the Custom House on King street, when seven of Captain Preston's company fired into the crowd, killing five men and wounding several others. Two of the victims were innocent bystanders. Two were sailors from ships lying in the harbour, and they, together with the remaining victim, a ropemaker, had been actively engaged in the affray. One of the sailors, a mulatto or half-breed Indian of gigantic stature, named Crispus Attucks, had been especially conspicuous. The slaughter of these five men secured in a moment what so many months of decorous protest had failed to accomplish. Much more serious bloodshed was imminent when Lieutenant-governor Hutchinson arrived upon the scene and promptly arrested the offending soldiers. The next day there was an immense meeting at the Old South, and Samuel Adams, at the head of a committee, came into the council chamber at the Town House, and in the name of three thousand freemen sternly commanded Hutchinson to remove the soldiers from the town. Before sunset they had all been withdrawn to the Castle. When the news reached the ears of

Parliament there was some talk of reinstating them in the town, but Colonel Barré cut short the discussion with the pithy question, "if the officers agreed in removing the soldiers to Castle William, what minister will dare to send them back to Boston?"

[Sidenote: Lord North, as prime minister removes all duties except on tea, 1770.]

Thus the so-called "Boston Massacre" wrought for the king a rebuff which he felt perhaps even more keenly than the repeal of the Stamp Act. Not only had his troops been peremptorily turned out of Boston, but his policy had for the moment weakened in its hold upon Parliament. In the summer of 1769 the assembly of Virginia adopted a very important series of resolutions condemning the policy of Great Britain and recommending united action on the part of the colonies in defence of their liberties. The governor then dissolved the assembly, whereupon its members met in convention at the Raleigh tavern and adopted a set of resolves prepared by Washington, strictly forbidding importations from England until the Townshend acts should be repealed. These resolves were generally adopted by the colonies, and presently the merchants of London, finding their trade falling off, petitioned Parliament to reconsider its policy. In January, 1770, Lord North became prime minister. In April all the duties were taken off, except the duty on tea, which the king insisted upon retaining, in order to avoid surrendering the principle at issue. The effect of even this partial concession was to weaken the spirit of opposition in America, and to create a division among the colonies. In July the merchants of New York refused to adhere any longer to the non-importation agreement except with regard to tea, and they began sending orders to England for various sorts of merchandise. Rhode Island and New Hampshire also broke the agreement. This aroused general indignation, and ships from the three delinquent colonies were driven from such ports as Boston and Charleston.

[Sidenote: Want of union.]

Union among the colonies was indeed only skin deep. The only thing which kept it alive was British aggression. Almost every colony had some bone of contention with its neighbours. At this moment New York and New Hampshire were wrangling over the possession of the Green Mountains, and guerrilla warfare was going on between Connecticut and Pennsylvania in the valley of Wyoming. It was hard to secure concerted action about anything. For two years after the withdrawal of troops from Boston there was a good deal of disturbance in different parts of the country; quarrels between governors and their assemblies were kept up with increasing bitterness; in North Carolina there was an insurrection against the governor which was suppressed only after a bloody battle near the Cape Fear river; in Rhode Island the revenue schooner Gaspee was seized and burned, and when an order came from the ministry requiring the offenders to be sent to England for trial, the chief-justice of Rhode Island, Stephen Hopkins, refused to obey the order. But amid all these disturbances there appeared nothing like concerted action on the part of the colonies. In June, 1772, Hutchinson said that the union of the colonies seemed to be broken, and he hoped it would not be renewed, for he believed it meant separation from the mother-country, and that he regarded as the worst of calamities.

CHAPTER V.THE CRISIS.

[Sidenote: Salaries of the judges.]

The surest way to renew and cement the union was to show that the ministry had not relaxed in its determination to enforce the principle of the Townshend acts. This was made clear in August, 1772, when it was ordered that in Massachusetts the judges should henceforth be paid by the crown. Popular excitement rose to fever heat, and the judges were threatened with impeachment should they dare accept a penny from the royal treasury. The turmoil was increased next year by the discovery in London of the package of letters which were made to support the unjust charge against Hutchinson and some of his friends that they had instigated and aided the most extreme measures of the ministry.

[Sidenote: Committees of Correspondence.]

In the autumn of 1772 Hutchinson refused to call an extra session of the assembly to consider what should be done about the judges. Samuel Adams then devised a scheme by which the towns of Massachusetts could consult with each other and agree upon some common course of action in case of emergencies. For this purpose each town was to appoint a standing committee, and as a great part of their work was necessarily done by letter they were called "committees of correspondence." This was the step that fairly organized the Revolution. It was by far the most important of all the steps that preceded the Declaration of Independence. The committees did their work with great efficiency and the governor had no means of stopping it. They were like an invisible legislature that was always in session and could never be dissolved; and when the old government fell they were able to administer affairs until a new government could be set up. In the spring of 1773 Virginia carried this work of organization a long step further, when Dabney Carr suggested and carried a motion calling for committees of correspondence between the several colonies. From this point it was a comparatively short step to a permanent Continental Congress.

It happened that these preparations were made just in time to meet the final act of aggression which brought on the Revolutionary War. The Americans had thus far successfully resisted the Townshend acts and secured the repeal of all the duties except on tea. As for tea they had plenty, but not from England; they smuggled it from Holland in spite of custom-houses and search-warrants. Clearly unless the Americans could be made to buy tea from England and pay the duty on it, the king must own himself defeated.

[Sidenote: Tea ships sent by the king, as a challenge.]

Since it appeared that they could not be forced into doing this, it remained to be seen if they could be tricked into doing it. A truly ingenious scheme was devised. Tea sent by the East India Company to America had formerly paid a duty in some British port on the way. This duty was now taken off, so that the price of the tea for America might be lowered. The company's tea thus became so cheap that the American merchant could buy a pound of it and pay the threepence duty beside for less than it cost him to smuggle a pound of tea from Holland. It was supposed that the Americans would of course buy the tea which they could get most cheaply, and would thus be beguiled into submission to that principle of taxation which they had hitherto resisted. Ships laden with tea were accordingly sent in the autumn of 1773 to Boston, New York, Philadelphia, and Charleston; and consignees were appointed to receive the tea in each of these towns.

Under the guise of a commercial operation, this was purely a political trick. It was an insulting challenge to the American people, and merited the reception which they gave it. They would have shown themselves unworthy of their rich political heritage had they given it any other. In New York, Philadelphia, and Charleston mass-meetings of the people voted that the consignees should be ordered to resign their offices, and they did so. At Philadelphia the tea-ship was met and sent back to England before it had come within the jurisdiction of the custom-house. At Charleston the tea was landed, and as there was no one to receive it or pay the duty, it was thrown into a damp cellar and left there to spoil.

[Sidenote: How the challenge was received; the "Boston Tea Party," Dec. 16, 1773.]

In Boston things took a different turn. The stubborn courage of Governor Hutchinson prevented the consignees, two of whom were his own sons, from resigning; the ships arrived and were anchored under guard of a committee of citizens; if they were not unloaded within twenty days, the custom-house officers were empowered by law to seize them and unload them by force; and having once come within the jurisdiction of the custom-house, they could not go out to sea without a clearance from the collector or a pass from the governor. The situation was a difficult one, but it was most nobly met by the men of Massachusetts. The excitement was intense, but the proceedings were characterized from first to last by perfect quiet and decorum. In an earnest and solemn, almost prayerful spirit, the advice of all the towns in the commonwealth was sought, and the response was unanimous that the tea must on no account whatever be landed. Similar expressions of opinion came from other colonies, and the action of Massachusetts was awaited with breathless interest. Many town-meetings were held in Boston, and the owner of the ships was ordered to take them away without unloading; but the collector contrived to fritter away the time until the nineteenth day, and then refused a clearance. On the next day, the 16th of December, 1773, seven thousand people were assembled in town-meeting in and around the Old South Meeting-House, while the owner of the ships was sent out to the governor's house at Milton to ask for a pass. It was nightfall when he returned without it, and there was then but one thing to be done. By sunrise next morning the revenue officers would board the ships and unload their cargoes, the consignees would go to the custom-house and pay the duty, and the king's scheme would have been crowned with success. The only way to prevent this was to rip open the tea-chests and spill their contents into the sea, and this was done, according to a preconcerted plan and without the slightest uproar or disorder, by a small party of men disguised as Indians. Among them were some of the best of the townsfolk, and the chief manager of the proceedings was Samuel Adams. The destruction of the tea has often been spoken of, especially by British historians, as a "riot," but nothing could have been less like a riot. It was really the deliberate action of the commonwealth of Massachusetts, and the only fitting reply to the king's insulting trick. It was hailed with delight throughout the thirteen colonies, and there is nothing in our whole history of which an educated American should feel more proud.

[Sidenote: The Retaliatory Acts, April, 1774.]

The effect upon the king and his friends was maddening, and events were quickly brought to a crisis. In spite of earnest opposition retaliatory acts were passed through Parliament in April, 1774. One of these was the Port Bill, for shutting up the port of Boston and stopping its trade until the people should be starved and frightened into paying for the tea that had been thrown overboard. Another was the Regulating Act, by which the charter of Massachusetts was annulled, its free government swept away, and a military governor appointed with despotic power like Andros. These acts were to go into operation on the 1st of June, and on that day Governor Hutchinson sailed for England, in the vain hope of persuading the king to adopt a milder policy. It was not long before his property was confiscated, like that of other Tories, and after six years of exile he died in London. The new governor, Thomas Gage, who had long been commander of the military forces in America, was a mild and pleasant man without much strength of character. His presence was endured but his authority was not recognized in Massachusetts. Troops were now quartered again in Boston, but they could not prevent the people from treating the Regulating Act with open contempt. Courts organized under that act were prevented from sitting, and councillors were compelled to resign their places. The king's authority was everywhere quietly but doggedly defied. At the same time the stoppage of business in Boston was the cause of much distress which all the colonies sought to relieve by voluntary contributions of food and other needed articles.

[Sidenote: Continental Congress meets, Sept. 1774.]

The events of the last twelve months had gone further than anything before toward awakening a sentiment of union among the people of the colonies. It was still a feeble sentiment, but it was strong enough to make them all feel that Boston was suffering in the common cause. The system of corresponding committees now ripened into the Continental Congress, which held its first meeting at Philadelphia in September, 1774. Among the delegates were Samuel and John Adams, Robert Livingston, John Rutledge, John Dickinson, Samuel Chase, Edmund Pendleton, Richard Henry Lee, Patrick Henry, and George Washington. Their action was cautious and conservative. They confined themselves for the present to trying the effect of a candid statement of grievances, and drew up a Declaration of Rights and other papers, which were pronounced by Lord Chatham unsurpassed for ability in any age or country. In Parliament, however, the king's friends were becoming all-powerful, and the only effect produced by these papers was to goad them toward further attempts at coercion. Massachusetts was declared to be in a state of rebellion, as in truth she was.

[Sidenote: The Suffolk Resolves, Sept. 1774.]

While Samuel Adams was at Philadelphia, the lead in Boston was taken by his friend Dr. Warren. In a county convention held at Milton in September, Dr. Warren drew up a series of resolves which fairly set on foot the Revolution. They declared that the Regulating Act was null and void, and that a king who violates the chartered rights of his subjects forfeits their allegiance; they directed the collectors of taxes to refuse to pay the money collected to Gage's treasurer; and they threatened retaliation in case Gage should venture to arrest any one for political reasons. These bold resolves were adopted by the convention and sanctioned by the Continental Congress. Next month the people of Massachusetts formed a provisional government, and began organizing a militia and collecting military stores at Concord and other inland towns.

[Sidenote: Battle of Lexington, April 19, 1775.]

General Gage's position at this time was a trying one for a man of his temperament. In an unguarded moment he had assured the king that four regiments ought to be enough to bring Massachusetts into an attitude of penitence. Now Massachusetts was in an attitude of rebellion, and he realized that he had not troops enough to command the situation. People in England were blaming him for not doing something, and late in the winter he received a positive order to arrest Samuel Adams and his friend John Hancock, then at the head of the new provisional government of Massachusetts, and send them to England to be tried for high treason. On the 18th of April, 1775, these gentlemen were staying at a friend's house in Lexington; and Gage that evening sent out a force of 800 men to seize the military stores accumulated at Concord, with instructions to stop on the way at Lexington and arrest Adams and Hancock. But Dr. Warren divined the purpose of the movement, and his messenger, Paul Revere, succeeded in forewarning the people, so that by the time the troops arrived at Lexington the birds were flown. The soldiers fired into a company of militia on Lexington common and slew eight or ten of their number; but by the time they reached Concord the country was fairly aroused and armed yeomanry were coming upon the scene by hundreds. In a sharp skirmish the British were defeated and, without having accomplished any of the objects of their expedition, began their retreat toward Boston, hotly pursued by the farmers who fired from behind walls and trees after the Indian fashion. A reinforcement of 1200 men at Lexington saved the routed troops from destruction, but the numbers of their assailants grew so rapidly that even this larger force barely succeeded in escaping capture. At sunset the British reached Charlestown after a march which was a series of skirmishes, leaving nearly 300 of their number killed or wounded along the road. By that time yeomanry from twenty-three townships had joined in the pursuit. The alarm spread like wildfire through New England, and fresh bands of militia arrived every hour. Within three days Israel Putnam and Benedict Arnold had come from Connecticut and John Stark from New Hampshire, a cordon of 16,000 men was drawn around Boston, and the siege of that town was begun.

[Sidenote: Capture of Ticonderoga, May 10, 1775.]

[Sidenote: Washington appointed to command the army, June 15, 1775.]

[Sidenote: Charles Lee.]

The belligerent feeling in New England had now grown so strong as to show itself in an act of offensive warfare. On the 10th of May, just three weeks after Lexington, the fortresses at Ticonderoga and Crown Point, controlling the line of communication between New York and Canada, were surprised and captured by men from the Green Mountains and Connecticut valley under Ethan Allen and Seth Warner. The Congress, which met on that same day at Philadelphia, showed some reluctance in sanctioning an act so purely offensive; but in its choice of a president the spirit of defiance toward Great Britain was plainly shown. John Hancock, whom the British commander-in-chief was under stringent orders to arrest and send over to England to be tried for treason, was chosen to that eminent position on the 24th of May. This showed that the preponderance of sentiment in the country was in favour of supporting the New England colonies in the armed struggle into which they had drifted. This was still further shown two days later, when Congress in the name of the "United Colonies of America" assumed the direction of the rustic army of New England men engaged in the siege of Boston. As Congress was absolutely penniless and had no power to lay taxes, it proceeded to borrow £6000 for the purchase of gunpowder. It called for ten companies of riflemen from Virginia, Maryland, and Pennsylvania, to reinforce what was henceforth known as the Continental army; and on the 15th of June it appointed George Washington commander-in-chief. The choice of Washington was partly due to the general confidence in his ability and in his lofty character. In the French War he had won a military reputation higher than that of any other American, and he was already commander-in-chief of the forces of Virginia. But the choice was also partly due to sound political reasons. The Massachusetts leaders, especially Samuel Adams and his cousin John, were distrusted by some people as extremists and fire-eaters. They wished to bring about a declaration of independence, for they believed it to be the only possible cure for the evils of the time. The leaders in other colonies, upon which the hand of the British government had not borne so heavily, had not yet advanced quite so far as this. Most of them believed that the king could be brought to terms; they did not realize that he would never give way because it was politically as much a life and death struggle for him as for them. Washington was not yet clearly in favour of independence, nor was Jefferson, who a twelvemonth hence was to be engaged in writing the Declaration. It is doubtful if any of the leading men as yet agreed with the Adamses, except Dr. Franklin, who had just returned from England after his ten years' stay there, and knew very well how little hope was to be placed in conciliatory measures. The Adamses, therefore, like wise statesmen, were always on their guard lest circumstances should drive Massachusetts in the path of rebellion faster than the sister colonies were likely to keep pace with her. This was what the king above all things wished, and by the same token it was what they especially dreaded and sought to avoid. To appoint George Washington to the chief command was to go a long way toward irrevocably committing Virginia to the same cause with Massachusetts, and John Adams was foremost in urging the appointment. Its excellence was obvious to every one, and we hear of only two persons that were dissatisfied. One of these was John Hancock, who coveted military distinction and was vain enough to think himself fit for almost any position. The other was Charles Lee, a British officer who had served in America in the French War and afterward wandered about Europe as a soldier of fortune. He had returned to America in 1773 in the hope of playing a leading part here. He set himself up as an authority on military questions, and pretended to be a zealous lover of liberty. He was really an unprincipled charlatan for whom, the kindest thing that can be said is that perhaps he was slightly insane. He had hoped to be appointed to the chief command, and was disgusted when he found himself placed second among the four major-generals. The first major-general was Artemas Ward of Massachusetts; the third was Philip Schuyler of New York; the fourth was Israel Putnam of Connecticut. Eight brigadier-generals were appointed, among whom we may here mention Richard Montgomery of New York, William Heath of Massachusetts, John Sullivan of New Hampshire, and Nathanael Greene of Rhode Island. The adjutant-general, Horatio Gates, was an Englishman who had served in the French War, and since then had lived in Virginia.

[Sidenote: Battle of Bunker Hill, June 17, 1775.]

While Congress was appointing officers and making regulations for the Continental army, reinforcements for the British had landed in Boston, making their army 10,000 strong. The new troops were commanded by General William Howe, a Whig who disapproved of the king's policy. With him came Sir Henry Clinton and John Burgoyne, who were more in sympathy with the king. Howe and Burgoyne were members of Parliament. On the arrival of these reinforcements Gage prepared to occupy the heights in Charlestown known as Breed's and Bunker's hills. These heights commanded Boston, so that hostile batteries placed there would make it necessary for the British to evacuate the town. On the night of June 16, the Americans anticipated Gage in seizing the heights, and began erecting fortifications on Breed's Hill. It was an exposed position for the American force, which might easily have been cut off and captured if the British had gone around by sea and occupied Charlestown Neck in the rear. The British preferred to storm the American works. In two desperate assaults, on the afternoon of the 17th, they were repulsed with the loss of one-third of their number; and the third assault succeeded only because the Americans were not supplied with powder. By driving the Americans back to Winter Hill, the British won an important victory and kept their hold upon Boston. The moral effect of the battle, however, was in favour of the Americans, for it clearly indicated that under proper circumstances they might exhibit a power of resistance which the British would find it impossible to overcome. It was with George III. as with Pyrrhus: he could not afford to win many victories at such cost, for his supply of soldiers for America was limited, and his only hope of success lay in inflicting heavy blows. In winning Bunker Hill his troops were only holding their own; the siege of Boston was not raised for a moment.

The practical effect upon the British army was to keep it quiet for several months. General Howe, who presently superseded Gage, was a brave and well-trained soldier, but slothful in temperament. His way was to strike a blow, and then wait to see what would come of it, hoping no doubt that political affairs might soon take such a turn as to make it unnecessary to go on with this fratricidal war. This was fortunate for the Americans, for when Washington took command of the army at Cambridge on the 3d of July, he saw that little or nothing could be done with that army until it should be far better organized, disciplined, and equipped, and in such work he found enough to occupy him for several months.

[Sidenote: Last petition to the king; and its answer.]

[Illustration: Invasion of Canada by Montgomery and Arnold.]

Meanwhile Congress, at the instance of John Dickinson of Pennsylvania and John Jay of New York, decided to try the effect of one more candid statement of affairs, in the form of a petition to the king. This paper reached London on the 14th of August, but the king refused to receive it, although it was signed by the delegates as separate individuals and not as members of an unauthorized or revolutionary body. His only answer was a proclamation dated August 23, in which he called for volunteers to aid in putting down the rebellion in America. At the same time he opened negotiations with the landgrave of Hesse-Cassel, the duke of Brunswick, and other petty German princes, and succeeded in hiring 20,000 troops to be sent to fight against his American subjects. When the news of this reached America it produced a profound effect. Perhaps nothing done in that year went so far toward destroying the lingering sentiment of loyalty.

[Sidenote: Americans invade Canada, Aug., 1775--June, 1776.]

In the spring Congress had hesitated about encouraging offensive operations. In the course of the summer it was ascertained that the governor of Canada, Sir Guy Carleton, was planning an invasion of northern New York and hoping to obtain the coöperation of the Six Nations and the Tories of the Mohawk valley. Congress accordingly decided to forestall him by invading

Canada. Two lines of invasion were adopted. Montgomery descended Lake Champlain with 2000 men, and after a campaign of two months captured Montreal on the 12th of November. At the same time Benedict Arnold and Daniel Morgan set out from Cambridge with 1200 men, and made their way through the wilderness of Maine, up the valley of the Kennebec and down that of the Chaudière, coming out upon the St. Lawrence opposite Quebec on the 13th of November. This long march through the primeval forest and over rugged and trackless mountains was one of the most remarkable exploits of the war. It cost the lives of 200 men, but besides this the rear-guard gave out and went back to Cambridge, so that when Arnold reached Quebec he had only 700 men, too few for an attack upon the town. After Montgomery joined him, it was decided to carry the works by storm, but in the unsuccessful assault on December 31, Montgomery was killed, Arnold disabled, and Morgan taken prisoner. During the winter Carleton was reinforced until he was able to recapture Montreal. The Americans were gradually driven back, and by June, 1776, had retreated to Crown Point. Carleton then resumed his preparations for invading New York.

[Sidenote: Washington takes Boston, March 17, 1776.]

While the northern campaign was progressing thus unfavourably, the British were at length driven from Boston. Howe had unaccountably neglected to occupy Dorchester heights, which commanded the town; and Washington, after waiting till a sufficient number of heavy guns could be collected, advanced on the night of March 4 and occupied them with 2000 men. His position was secure. The British had no alternative but to carry it by storm or retire from Boston. Not caring to repeat the experiment of Bunker Hill, they embarked on the 17th of March and sailed to Halifax, where they busied themselves in preparations for an expedition against New York. Late in April Washington transferred his headquarters to New York, where he was able to muster about 8000 men for its defence. Thus the line of the Hudson river was now threatened with attack at both its upper and lower ends.

[Sidenote: Lord Dunmore in Virginia.]

This change in the seat of war marks the change that had come over the political situation. It was no longer merely a rebellious Massachusetts that must be subdued; it was a continental Union that must be broken up. During the winter and spring the sentiment in favour of a declaration of independence had rapidly grown in strength. In November, 1775, Lord Dunmore, royal governor of Virginia, sought to intimidate the revolutionary party by a proclamation offering freedom to such slaves as would enlist under the king's banner. This aroused the country against Dunmore, and in December he was driven from Norfolk and took refuge in a ship of war. On New Year's Day he bombarded the town and laid it in ashes from one end to the other. This violence rapidly made converts to the revolutionary party, and further lessons were learned from the experience of their neighbours in North Carolina.

[Sidenote: North Carolina and Virginia.]

That colony was the scene of fierce contests between Whigs and Tories. As early as May 31, 1775, the patriots of Mecklenburg county had adopted resolutions pointing toward independence and forwarded them to their delegates in Congress, who deemed it impolitic, however, to lay them before that body. Josiah Martin, royal governor of North Carolina, was obliged to flee on board ship in July. He busied himself with plans for the complete subjugation of the southern colonies, and corresponded with the government in London, as well as with his Tory friends ashore. In pursuance of these plans Sir Henry Clinton, with 2000 men, was detached in January, 1776, from the army in Boston, and sent to the North Carolina coast; a fleet under Sir Peter Parker was sent from Ireland to meet him; and a force of 1600 Tories was gathered to assist him as soon as he should arrive. But the scheme utterly failed. The fleet was buffeted by adverse winds and did not arrive; the Tories were totally defeated on February 27 in a sharp fight at Moore's Creek; and Clinton, thus deprived of his allies, deemed it most prudent for a while to keep his troops on shipboard. On the 12th of April the patriots of North Carolina instructed their delegates in Congress to concur with other delegates in a declaration of independence. On the 14th of May Virginia went further, and instructed her delegates to propose such a declaration. South Carolina, Georgia, and Rhode Island expressed a willingness to concur in any measures which Congress might think best calculated to promote the general welfare. In the course of May town-meetings throughout Massachusetts expressed opinions unanimously in favour of independence.

Massachusetts had already, as long ago as July, 1775, framed a new government in which the king was not recognized; and her example had been followed by New Hampshire in January, 1776, and by South Carolina in March. Now on the 15th of May Congress adopted a resolution advising all the other colonies to form new governments, because the king had "withdrawn his protection" from the American people, and all governments deriving their powers from him were accordingly set aside as of no account. This resolution was almost equivalent to a declaration of independence, and it was adopted only after hot debate and earnest opposition from the middle colonies.

[Sidenote: Richard Henry Lee's motion in Congress.]

On the 7th of June, in accordance with the instructions of May 14 from Virginia, Richard Henry Lee submitted to Congress the following resolutions:--

"That these United Colonies are, and of right ought to be, free and independent States, that they are absolved from all allegiance to the British Crown, and that all political connection between them and the State of Great Britain is, and ought to be, totally dissolved;

"That it is expedient forthwith to take the most effectual measures for forming foreign alliances;

"That a plan of confederation be prepared and transmitted to the respective colonies for their consideration and approbation."

This motion of Virginia, in which Independence and Union went hand in hand, was at once seconded by Massachusetts, as represented by John Adams. It was opposed by John Dickinson and James Wilson of Pennsylvania, and by Robert Livingston of New York, on the ground that the people of the middle colonies were not yet ready to sever the connection with the mother country. As the result of the discussion it was decided to wait three weeks, in the hope of hearing from all those colonies which had not yet declared themselves.

The messages from those colonies came promptly enough. As for Connecticut and New Hampshire, there could be no doubt; and their declarations for independence, on the 14th and 15th of June respectively, were simply dilatory expressions of their sentiments. They were late, only because Connecticut had no need to form a new government at all, while New Hampshire had formed one as long ago as January. Their support of the proposed declaration of independence was already secured, and it was only in the formal announcement of it that they were somewhat belated. But with the middle colonies it was different. There the parties were more evenly balanced, and it was not until the last moment that the decision was clearly pronounced. This was not because they were less patriotic than the other colonies, but because their direct grievances were fewer, and up to this moment they had hoped that the quarrel was one which a change of ministry in Great Britain might adjust. In the earlier stages of the quarrel they had been ready enough to join hands with Massachusetts and Virginia. It was only on this irrevocable decision as to independence that they were slow to act.

[Sidenote: The middle colonies.]

But in the course of the month of June their responses to the invitation of Congress came in,-- from Delaware on the 14th, from New Jersey on the 22d, from Pennsylvania on the 24th, from Maryland on the 28th. This action of the middle colonies was avowedly based on the ground that, in any event, united action was the thing most to be desired; so that, whatever their individual preferences might be, they were ready to subordinate them to the interests of the whole country. The broad and noble spirit of patriotism shown in their resolves is worthy of no less credit than the bold action of the colonies which, under the stimulus of direct aggression, first threw down the gauntlet to George III.

On the 1st of July, when Lee's motion was taken up in Congress, all the colonies had been heard from except New York. The circumstances of this central colony were peculiar. We have already seen that the Tory party was especially strong in New York. Besides this, her position was more exposed to attack on all sides than that of any other state. As the military centre of the Union, her territory was sure to be the scene of the most desperate fighting. She was already threatened with invasion from Canada. As a frontier state she was exposed to the incursions of the terrible Iroquois, and as a sea-board state she was open to the attack of the British fleet. At that time, moreover, the population of New York numbered only about 170,000, and she ranked seventh among the thirteen colonies. The military problem was therefore much harder for New York than for Massachusetts or Virginia. Her risks were greater than those of any other colony. For these reasons the Whig party in New York found itself seriously hampered in its movements, and the 1st of July arrived before their delegates in Congress had been instructed how to vote on the question of independence.

[Sidenote: Difficulties in New York.]

Richard Henry Lee had been suddenly called home to Virginia by the illness of his wife, and so the task of defending his motion fell upon John Adams who had seconded it. His speech on that occasion was so able that Thomas Jefferson afterward spoke of him as "the Colossus of that debate." As Congress sat with closed doors and no report was made of the speech, we have no definite knowledge of its arguments. Fifty years afterwards, shortly after John Adams's death, Daniel Webster wrote an imaginary speech containing what in substance he *might* have said. The principal argument in opposition was made by John Dickinson, who thought that before the Americans finally committed themselves to a deadly struggle with Great Britain, they ought to establish some stronger government than the Continental Congress, and ought also to secure a promise of help from some such country as France. This advice was cautious, but it was not sound and practical. War had already begun, and if we had waited to agree upon some permanent kind of government before committing all the colonies to a formal defiance of Great Britain, there was great danger that the enemy might succeed in breaking up the Union before it was really formed. Besides, it is not likely that France would ever have decided to go to war in our behalf until we had shown that we were able to defend ourselves. It was now a time when the boldest advice was the safest.

[Sidenote: The Declaration of Independence, July 1 to 4, 1776.]

During this debate on the 1st of July Congress was sitting as a committee of the whole, and at the close of the day a preliminary vote was taken. Like all the votes in the Continental Congress, it was taken by colonies. The majority of votes in each delegation determined the vote of that colony. Each colony had one vote, and two-thirds of the whole number, or nine colonies against four, were necessary for a decision. On this occasion the New York delegates did not vote at all, because they had no instructions. One delegate from Delaware voted yea and another nay; the third delegate, Cæsar Rodney, had been down in the lower counties of his little state, arguing against the loyalists. A special messenger had been sent to hurry him back, but he had not yet arrived, and so the vote of Delaware was divided and lost. Pennsylvania declared in the negative by four votes against three. South Carolina also declared in the negative. The other nine colonies all voted in the affirmative, and so the resolution received just votes enough to carry it. A very little more opposition would have defeated it, and would probably have postponed the declaration for several weeks.

The next day Congress took the formal vote upon the resolution. Mr. Rodney had now arrived, so that the vote of Delaware was given in the affirmative. John Dickinson and Robert Morris stayed away, so that Pennsylvania was now secured for the affirmative by three votes against two. Though Dickinson and Morris were so slow to believe it necessary or prudent to declare independence, they were firm supporters of the declaration after it was made. Without Morris, indeed, it is hard to see how the Revolution could have succeeded. He was the great financier of his time, and his efforts in raising money for the support of our hard-pressed armies were wonderful.

When the turn of the South Carolina delegates came they changed their votes in order that the declaration might go forth to the world as the unanimous act of the American people. The question was thus settled on the 2d of July, and the next thing was to decide upon the form of the declaration, which Jefferson, who was weak in debate but strong with the pen, had already drafted. The work was completed on the 4th of July, when Jefferson's draft was adopted and published to the world. Five days afterward the state of New York declared her approval of these proceedings. The Rubicon was crossed, and the thirteen English colonies had become the United

States of America.

CHAPTER VI.THE STRUGGLE FOR THE CENTRE.

[Sidenote: Lord Cornwallis.]

While these things were going on at Philadelphia, the coast of South Carolina, as well as the harbour of New York, was threatened by the British fleet. When the delegates from South Carolina gave their votes on the question of independence, they did not know but the revolutionary government in Charleston might already have been taken captive or scattered in flight. After a stormy voyage Sir Peter Parker's squadron at length arrived off Cape Fear early in May, and joined Sir Henry Clinton. Along with Sir Peter came an officer worthy of especial mention. Charles, Earl Cornwallis, was then thirty-eight years old. He had long served with distinction in the British army, and had lately reached the grade of lieutenant-general. In politics he was a New Whig, and had on several occasions signified his disapproval of the king's policy toward America. As a commander his promptness and vigour contrasted strongly with the slothfulness of General Howe. Cornwallis was the ablest of the British generals engaged in the Revolutionary War, and among the public men of his time there were few, if any, more high-minded, disinterested, faithful, and pure. After the war was over, he won great fame as governor-general of India from 1786 to 1794. He was afterward raised to the rank of marquis and appointed lord-lieutenant of Ireland. In 1805 he was sent out again to govern India, and died there.

[Sidenote: Battle of Fort Moultrie, June 28, 1776.]

[Sidenote: Lord Howe's effort toward conciliation.]

On the arrival of the fleet it was decided to attack and capture Charleston, and overthrow the new government there. General Charles Lee was sent down by Congress to defend the city, but the South Carolina patriots proved quite able to take care of themselves. On Sullivan's Island in Charleston harbour Colonel William Moultrie built a low elastic fortress of palmetto logs supported by banks of sand and mounting several heavy guns. In the cannonade which took place on the 28th of June this rude structure escaped with little injury, while its guns inflicted such serious damage upon the fleet that the British were obliged to abandon for the present all thought of taking Charleston. In the course of July they sailed for New York harbour to reinforce General Howe. On the 12th of that month the general's brother, Richard, Lord Howe, arrived at Staten Island to take the chief command of the fleet. He was one of the ablest seamen of his time, and was a favourite with his sailors, by whom, on account of his swarthy complexion, he was familiarly known as "Black Dick." Lord Howe and his brother were authorized to offer terms to the Americans and endeavour to restore peace by negotiation. It was not easy, however, to find any one in America with whom to negotiate. Lord Howe was sincerely desirous of making peace and doing something to heal the troubles which had brought on the war; and he seems to have supposed that some good might be effected by private interviews with leading Americans. To send a message to Congress was, of course, not to be thought of; for that would be equivalent to recognizing Congress as a body entitled to speak for the American people. He brought with him an assurance of amnesty and pardon for all such rebels as would lay down their arms, and decided that it would be best to send it to the American commander; but as it was not proper to recognize the military rank which had been conferred upon Washington by a revolutionary body, he addressed his message to "George Washington, Esq.," as to a private citizen. When Washington refused to receive such a message, his lordship could think of no one else to approach except the royal governors. But they had all fled, except Governor Franklin of New Jersey, who was under close confinement in East Windsor, Connecticut. All British authority in the United States had disappeared, and there was no one for Lord Howe to negotiate with, unless he should bethink himself of some way of laying his case before Congress.

[Sidenote: Change in the British military plan, due to the union of the colonies in the Declaration of Independence.]

Military operations were now taken up in earnest by the British, and were briskly carried on for nearly six months. They were for the most part concentrated upon the state of New York. Before 1776 it was Massachusetts that was the chief object of military measures on the part of the British. That was the colony that since the summer of 1774 had defied the king's troops and set at naught the authority of Parliament; and the first object of the British was to make an example of that colony, to suppress the rebellion there, and to reinstate the royal government. The king believed that it would not take long to do this, and there is some reason for supposing that if he had succeeded in humbling Massachusetts, he would have been ready to listen to Hutchinson's request that the vindictive acts of April, 1774, should be repealed and the charter restored. At all events, he seems to have felt confident that things could soon be made so quiet that Hutchinson could return and resume the office of governor. If the king and his friends had not entertained such ill-founded hopes, they would not have been so ready to resort to violent measures. They made the fatal mistake of supposing that such a man as Samuel Adams represented only a small party and not the majority of the people. They had also supposed that the other colonies would not make common cause with Massachusetts. But now, before they had accomplished any of their objects, and while their troops had even been driven from Boston, they found that the rebellion had spread through the whole country. They had a belligerent government to confront, and must now enter upon the task of conquering the United States.

[Sidenote: Why the British concentrated their attack upon the state of New York.]

The first and most obvious method of attempting this was to strike at New York as the military centre. In such a plan everything seemed to favour the British. The state was comparatively weak in population and resources; a large proportion of the people were Tories; and close at hand on the frontier, which was then in the Mohawk valley, were the most formidable Indians on the continent. These Iroquois had long been under the influence of the famous Sir William Johnson, of Johnson Hall, near Schenectady, and his son Sir John Johnson. Their principal sachem, Joseph Brant, or Thayendanegea, was connected by the closest bonds of friendship with the Johnsons, and the latter were staunch Tories. It might reasonably be expected that the entire force of these Indians could be enlisted on the British side. The work for the regular army seemed thus to be reduced to the single problem of capturing the city of New York and obtaining full control of the Hudson river.

If this could be done, the United States would be cut in two. As the Americans had no ships of war, they could not dispute the British command of the water. There was no way in which the

New England states could hold communication with the South except across the southern part of the state of New York. To gain this central position would thus be to deal a fatal blow to the American cause, and it seemed to the British government that, with the forces now in the field, this ought easily to be accomplished. General Carleton was ready to come down from the north by way of Lake Champlain, with 12,000 men, and General Schuyler could scarcely muster half as many to oppose him. On Staten Island there were more than 25,000 British troops ready to attack New York, while Washington's utmost exertions had succeeded in getting together only about 18,000 men for the defence of the city. The American army was as yet very poor in organization and discipline, badly equipped, and scantily fed; and it seemed very doubtful whether it could long keep the field in the presence of superior forces.

[Sidenote: Washington's military genius.]

But in spite of all these circumstances, so favourable to the British, there was one obstacle to their success upon which at first they did not sufficiently reckon. That obstacle was furnished by the genius and character of the wonderful man who commanded the American army. In Washington were combined all the highest qualities of a general,--dogged tenacity of purpose, endless fertility in resource, sleepless vigilance, and unfailing courage. No enemy ever caught him unawares, and he never let slip an opportunity of striking back. He had a rare geographical instinct, always knew where the strongest position was, and how to reach it. He was a master of the art of concealing his own plan and detecting his adversary's. He knew better than to hazard everything upon the result of a single contest, and because of the enemy's superior force he was so often obliged to refuse battle that some of his impatient critics called him slow; but no general was ever quicker in dealing heavy blows when the proper moment arrived. He was neither unduly elated by victory nor discouraged by defeat. When all others lost heart he was bravest; and at the very moment when ruin seemed to stare him in the face, he was craftily preparing disaster and confusion for the enemy.

To the highest qualities of a military commander there were united in Washington those of a political leader. From early youth he possessed the art of winning men's confidence. He was simple without awkwardness, honest without bluntness, and endowed with rare discretion and tact. His temper was fiery and on occasion he could use pretty strong language, but anger or disappointment was never allowed to disturb the justice and kindness of his judgment. Men felt themselves safe in putting entire trust in his head and his heart, and they were never deceived. Thus he soon obtained such a hold upon the people as few statesmen have ever possessed. It was this grand character that, with his clear intelligence and unflagging industry, enabled him to lead the nation triumphantly through the perils of the Revolutionary War. He had almost every imaginable hardship to contend with,--envious rivals, treachery and mutiny in the camp, interference on the part of Congress, jealousies between the states, want of men and money; yet all these difficulties he vanquished. Whether victorious or defeated on the field, he baffled the enemy in the first year's great campaign and in the second year's, and then for four years more upheld the cause until heart-sickening delay was ended in glorious triumph. It is very doubtful if without Washington the struggle for independence would have succeeded as it did. Other men were important, he was indispensable.

[Sidenote: Battle of Long Island, Aug. 27, 1776.]

The first great campaign began, as might have been expected, with defeat on the field. In order to keep possession of the city of New York it was necessary to hold Brooklyn Heights. That was a dangerous position for an American force, because it was entirely separated from New York by deep water, and could thus be cut off from the rest of the American army by the enemy's fleet. It was necessary, however, for Washington either to occupy Brooklyn Heights or to give up the city of New York without a struggle. But the latter course was out of the question. It would never do to abandon the Whigs in New York to the tender mercies of the Tories, without at least one good fight. So the position in Brooklyn must be fortified, and there was perhaps one chance in a hundred that, through some blunder of the enemy, we might succeed in holding it. Accordingly 9000 men were stationed on Brooklyn Heights under Putnam, who threw forward about half of this force, under Sullivan and Stirling, to defend the southern approaches through the rugged country between Gowanus bay and Bedford. On the 22d of August General Howe crossed from Staten Island to Gravesend bay with 20,000 men, and on the 27th he defeated Sullivan and Stirling in what has ever since been known as the battle of Long Island. About 400 men were killed and wounded on each side, and 1000 Americans, including both generals, were taken captive. A more favourable result for the Americans was not to be expected, as the British outnumbered them four to one, and could therefore march where they pleased and turn the American flank without incurring the slightest risk. The wonder is, not that 5000 half-trained soldiers were defeated by 20,000 veterans, but that they should have given General Howe a good day's work in defeating them.

[Sidenote: Washington's skilful retreat.]

The American forces were now withdrawn into their works on Brooklyn Heights, and Howe advanced to besiege them. During the next two days Washington collected boats and on the night of the 29th conveyed the army across the East River to New York. With the enemy's fleet patrolling the harbour and their army watching the works, this was a most remarkable performance. To this day one cannot understand, unless on the supposition that the British were completely dazed and moonstruck, how Washington could have done it.

[Sidenote: Howe takes New York, Sept. 15, 1776.]

People were much disheartened by the defeat on Long Island and the immediate prospect of losing New York. Lord Howe turned his thoughts once more to negotiation, and at length, on September 11, succeeded in obtaining an informal interview with Franklin, John Adams, and Edward Rutledge. But nothing was accomplished, and seventeen eventful months elapsed before the British again seriously tried negotiation. General Howe had extended his lines northward, and on the 15th his army crossed the East River in boats, and landed near the site of Thirty-Fourth street. On the same day Washington completed the work of evacuating the city. His army was drawn up across the island from the mouth of Harlem river to Fort Washington, and over on the Jersey side of the Hudson, opposite Fort Washington, a detachment occupied Fort Lee. It was hoped that these two forts would be able to prevent British ships from going up the Hudson river, but this hope soon proved to be delusive.

On the 16th General Howe tried to break through the centre of Washington's position at Harlem Heights, but after losing 300 men he gave up the attempt, and spent the next three weeks in studying the situation. A sad incident came now to remind the people of the sternness of military law. Nathan Hale, a young graduate of Yale College, captain of a company of Connecticut rangers, had been for several days within the British lines gathering information. Just as he had accomplished his purpose, and was on the point of departing with his memoranda, he was arrested as a spy and hanged next morning, lamenting on the gallows that he had but one life to lose for his country.

[Sidenote: Battle of White Plains, Oct. 28, 1776.]

As Howe deemed it prudent not to attack Washington in front, he tried to get around into his rear, and began on October 12 by landing a large force at Throg's Neck, in the Sound. But Washington baffled him by changing front, swinging his left wing northward as far as White Plains. After further reflection Howe decided to try a front attack once more; on the 28th he assaulted the position at White Plains, and carried one of the outposts, losing twice as many men as the Americans. Not wishing to continue the fight at such a disadvantage he paused again, and Washington improved the occasion by retiring to a still stronger position at Northcastle. These movements had separated Washington's main body from his right wing at Forts Washington and Lee, and Howe now changed his plan. Desisting from the attempt against the American main body, he moved southward against this exposed wing.

A sad catastrophe now followed, which showed how many obstacles Washington had to contend with. It was known that Carleton's army was on the way from Canada. Congress was nervously afraid of losing its hold upon the Hudson river, and Washington accordingly selected West Point as the strongest position upon the river, to be fortified and defended at all hazards. He sent Heath, with 3000 men, to hold the Highland passes, and went up himself to inspect the situation and give directions about the new fortifications. He left 7000 of his main body at Northcastle, in charge of Lee, who had just returned from South Carolina. He sent 5000, under Putnam, across the river to Hackensack; and ordered Greene, who had some 5000 men at Forts Washington and Lee, to prepare to evacuate both those strongholds and join his forces to Putnam's.

If these orders had been carried out, Howe's movement against Fort Washington would have accomplished but little, for on reaching that place, he would have found nothing but empty works, as at Brooklyn. The American right wing would have been drawn together at Hackensack, and the whole army could have been concentrated on either bank of the great river, as the occasion might seem to require. If Howe should aim at the Highlands, it could be kept close to the river and cover all the passes. If, on the other hand, Howe should threaten the Congress at Philadelphia, the whole army could be collected in New Jersey to hold him in check.

[Sidenote: Howe takes Fort Washington, Nov. 16, 1776.]

But Washington's orders were not obeyed. Congress was so uneasy that it sent word to Greene to hold both his forts as long as he could. Accordingly he strengthened the garrison at Fort Washington, just in time for Howe to overwhelm and capture it, on the 16th of November, after an obstinate resistance. In killed and wounded the British loss was three times as great as that of the garrison, but the Americans were in no condition to afford the loss of 8000 men taken prisoners. It was a terrible blow. On the 19th Greene barely succeeded in escaping from Fort Lee, with his remaining 2000 men, but without his cannon and stores.

[Sidenote: Treachery of Charles Lee.]

Bad as the situation was, however, it did not become really alarming until it was complicated with the misconduct of General Lee. Washington had returned from West Point on the 14th, too late to prevent the catastrophe; but after all it was only necessary for Lee's wing of the army to cross the river, and there would be a solid force of 14,000 men on the Jersey side, able to confront the enemy on something like equal terms, for Howe had to keep a good many of his troops in New York. On the 17th Washington ordered Lee to come over and join him; but Lee disobeyed, and in spite of repeated orders from Washington he stayed at Northcastle till the 2d of December. General Ward had some time since resigned, so that Lee now ranked next to Washington. A good many people were finding fault with the latter for losing the 3000 men at Fort Washington, although, as we have seen, that was not his fault but the fault of Congress. Lee now felt that if Washington were ruined, he would surely become his successor in the command of the army, and so, instead of obeying his orders, he spent his time in writing letters calculated to injure him.

[Sidenote: Washington's retreat through New Jersey.]

Lee's disobedience thus broke the army in two, and did more for the British than they had been able to do for themselves since they started from Staten Island. It was the cause of Washington's flight through New Jersey, ending on the 8th of December, when he put himself behind the Delaware river, with scarcely 3000 men. Here was another difficulty. The American soldiers were enlisted for short terms, and when they were discouraged, as at present, they were apt to insist upon going home as soon as their time had expired. It was generally believed that Washington's army would thus fall to pieces within a few days. Howe did not think it worth while to be at the trouble of collecting boats wherewith to follow him across the Delaware. Congress fled to Baltimore. People in New Jersey began taking the oath of allegiance to the crown. Howe received the news that he had been knighted for his victory on Long Island, and he returned to New York to celebrate the occasion.

[Sidenote: Arnold's naval battle at Valcour Island, Oct. 11, 1776.]

While the case looked so desperate for Washington, events at the north had taken a less unfavourable turn. Carleton had embarked on Lake Champlain early in the autumn with his fine army and fleet. Arnold had fitted up a small fleet to oppose his advance, and on the 11th of October there had been a fierce naval battle between the two near Valcour Island, in which Arnold was defeated, while Carleton suffered serious damage. The British general then advanced upon Ticonderoga, but suddenly made up his mind that the season was too late for operations in that latitude. The resistance he had encountered seems to have made him despair of achieving any speedy success in that quarter, and on the 3d of November he started back for Canada. This retreat relieved General Schuyler at Albany of immediate cause for anxiety, and presently he detached seven regiments to go southward to Washington's assistance.

[Sidenote: Charles Lee is captured by British dragoons, Dec. 13, 1776.]

On the 2d of December Lee crossed the Hudson with 4000 men, and proceeded slowly to Morristown. Just what he designed to do was never known, but clearly he had no intention of going beyond the Delaware to assist Washington, whom he believed to be ruined. Perhaps he thought Morristown a desirable position to hold, as it certainly was. Whatever his plans may have been, they were nipped in the bud. For some unknown reason he passed the night of the 12th at an unguarded tavern, about four miles from his army; and there he was captured next morning by a party of British dragoons, who carried him off to their camp at Princeton. The dragoons were very gleeful over this unexpected exploit, but really they could not have done the Americans a greater service than to rid them of such a worthless creature. The capture of Lee came in the nick of time, for it set free his men to go to the aid of Washington. Even after this force and that sent by Schuyler had reached the commander-in-chief, he found he had only 6000 men fit for duty.

[Sidenote: Battle of Trenton, Dec. 26, 1776.]

[Illustration: Washington's Campaigns IN NEW JERSEY & PENNSYLVANIA.]

With this little force Washington instantly took the offensive. It was the turning-point in his career and in the history of the Revolutionary War. On Christmas, 1776, and the following nine days, all Washington's most brilliant powers were displayed. The British centre, 10,000 strong, lay at Princeton. The principal generals, thinking the serious business of the war ended, had gone to New York. An advanced party of Hessians, 1000 strong, was posted on the bank of the Delaware at Trenton, and another one lower down, at Burlington. Washington decided to attack both these outposts, and arranged his troops accordingly, but when Christmas night arrived, the river was filled with great blocks of floating ice, and the only division which succeeded in crossing was the one that Washington led in person. It was less than 2500 in number, but the moment had come when the boldest course was the safest. By daybreak Washington had surprised the Hessians at Trenton and captured them all. The outpost at Burlington, on hearing the news, retreated to Princeton. By the 31st Washington had got all his available force across to Trenton. Some of them were raw recruits just come in to replace others who had just gone home. At this critical moment the army was nearly helpless for want of money, and on New Year's morning Robert Morris was knocking at door after door in Philadelphia, waking up his friends to borrow the fifty thousand dollars which he sent off to Trenton before noon. The next day Cornwallis arrived at Princeton, and taking with him all the army, except a rear-guard of 2000 men left to protect his communications, came on toward Trenton.

When he reached that town, late in the afternoon, he found Washington entrenched behind a small creek just south of the town, with his back toward the Delaware river. "Oho!" said Cornwallis, "at last we have run down the old fox, and we will bag him in the morning." He sent back to Princeton, and ordered the rear-guard to come up. He expected next morning to cross the creek above Washington's right, and then press him back against the broad and deep river, and compel him to surrender. Cornwallis was by no means a careless general, but he seems to have gone to bed on that memorable night and slept the sleep of the just.

[Sidenote: Battle of Princeton, Jan. 3, 1777.]

Washington meanwhile was wide awake. He kept his front line noisily at work digging and entrenching, and made a fine show with his campfires. Then he marched his army to the right and across the creek, and got around Cornwallis's left wing and into his rear, and so went on gayly toward Princeton. At daybreak he encountered the British rear-guard, fought a sharp battle with it and sent it flying, with the loss of one-fourth of its number. The booming guns aroused Cornwallis too late. To preserve his communications with New York, he was obliged to retreat with all haste upon New Brunswick, while Washington's victorious army pushed on and occupied the strong position at Morristown.

There was small hope of dislodging such a general from such a position. But to leave Washington in possession of Morristown was to resign to him the laurels of this half-year's work. For that position guarded the Highlands of the Hudson on the one hand, and the roads to Philadelphia on the other. Except that the British had taken the city of New York--which from the start was almost a foregone conclusion--they were no better off than in July when Lord Howe had landed on Staten Island. In nine days the tables had been completely turned. The attack upon an outpost had developed into a campaign which quite retrieved the situation. The ill-timed interference of Congress, which had begun the series of disasters, was remedied; the treachery of Lee was checkmated; and the cause of American Independence, which on Christmas Eve had seemed hopeless, was now fairly set on its feet. Earlier successes had been local; this was continental. Seldom has so much been done with such slender means.

[Sidenote: Effects of the campaign, in Europe.]

The American war had begun to awaken interest in Europe, especially in France, whither Franklin, with Silas Deane and Arthur Lee, had been sent to seek for military aid. The French government was not yet ready to make an alliance with the United States, but money and arms were secretly sent over to Congress. Several young French nobles had asked the king's permission to go to America, but it was refused, and for the sake of keeping up appearances the refusal had something of the air of a reprimand. The king did not wish to offend Great Britain prematurely. One of these nobles was Lafayette, then eighteen years of age, who fitted up a ship at his own expense, and sailed from Bordeaux in April, 1777, in spite of the royal prohibition, taking with him Kalb and other officers. Lafayette and Kalb, with the Poles, Kosciuszko and Pulaski, who had come some time before, and the German Steuben, who came in the following December, were the five most eminent foreigners who received commissions in the Continental army.

[Sidenote: Difficulty in raising an army.]

During the winter season at Morristown the efforts of Washington were directed toward the establishment of a regular army to be kept together for three years or so long as the war should last. Hitherto the military preparations of Congress had been absurdly weak. Squads of militia had been enlisted for terms of three or six months, as if there were any likelihood of the war being ended within such a period. While the men thus kept coming and going, it was difficult either to maintain discipline or to carry out any series of military operations. Accordingly

Congress now proceeded to call upon the states for an army of 80,000 men to serve during the war. The enlisting was to be done by the states, but the money was to be furnished by Congress. Not half that number of men were actually obtained. The Continental army was larger in 1777 than in any other year, but the highest number it reached was only 34,820. In addition to these about 34,000 militia turned out in the course of the year. An army of 80,000 would have taken about the same proportion of all the fighting men in the country as an army of 1,000,000 in our great Civil War. Now in our Civil War the Union army grew with the occasion until it numbered more than 1,000,000. But in the Revolutionary War the Continental army was not only never equal to the occasion, but it kept diminishing till in 1781 it numbered only 13,292. This was because the Continental Congress had no power to enforce its decrees. It could only *ask* for troops and it could only *ask* for money. It found just the same difficulty in getting anything that the British ministry and the royal governors used to find,--the very same difficulty that led Grenville to devise the Stamp Act. Everything had to be talked over in thirteen different legislatures, one state would wait to see what another was going to do, and meanwhile Washington was expected to fight battles before his army was fit to take the field. Something was gained, no doubt, by Congress furnishing the money. But as Congress could not tax anybody, it had no means of raising a revenue, except to beg, borrow, or issue its promissory notes, the so-called Continental paper currency.

[Sidenote: The British plan for conquering New York in 1777.]

While Congress was trying to raise an adequate army, the British ministry laid its plans for the summer campaign. The conquest of the state of New York must be completed at all hazards; and to this end a threefold system of movements was devised:--

First, the army in Canada was to advance upon Ticonderoga, capture it, and descend the Hudson as far as Albany. This work was now entrusted to General Burgoyne.

Secondly, in order to make sure of efficient support from the Six Nations and the Tories of the frontier, a small force under Colonel Barry St. Leger was to go up the St. Lawrence to Lake Ontario, land at Oswego, and march down the Mohawk valley to reinforce Burgoyne on the Hudson.

Thirdly, after leaving a sufficient force to hold the city of New York, the main army, under Sir William Howe, was to ascend the Hudson, capture the forts in the Highlands, and keep on to Albany, so as to effect a junction with Burgoyne and St. Leger.

It was thought that such an imposing display of military force would make the Tory party supreme in New York, put an end to all resistance there, and effectually cut the United States in two. Then if the southern states on the one hand and the New England states on the other did not hasten to submit, they might afterward be attacked separately and subdued.

In this plan the ministry made the fatal mistake of underrating the strength of the feeling which, from one end of the United States to the other, was setting itself every day more and more decidedly against the Tories and in favour of independence. This feeling grew as fast as the anti-slavery feeling grew among the northern people during our Civil War. In 1861 President Lincoln thought it necessary to rebuke his generals who were too forward in setting free the slaves of persons engaged in rebellion against the United States. In 1862 he announced his purpose to emancipate all such slaves; and then it took less than three years to put an end to slavery forever. It was just so with the sentiment in favour of separation from Great Britain. In July, 1775, Thomas Jefferson expressly declared that the Americans had not raised armies with any intention of declaring their independence of the mother-country. In July, 1776, the Declaration of Independence, written by Jefferson, was proclaimed to the world, though the consent of the middle colonies and of South Carolina seemed somewhat reluctant. By the summer of 1777 the Tories were almost everywhere in a hopeless minority. Every day of warfare, showing Great Britain more and more clearly as an enemy to be got rid of, diminished their strength; so that, even in New York and South Carolina, where they were strongest, it would not do for the British ministry to count too much upon any support they might give.

It was natural enough that King George and his ministers should fail to understand all this, but their mistake was their ruin. If they had understood that Burgoyne's march from Lake Champlain to the Hudson river was to be a march through a country thoroughly hostile, perhaps they would not have been so ready to send him on such a dangerous expedition. It would have been much easier and safer to have sent his army by sea to New York, to reinforce Sir William Howe. Threatening movements might have been made by some of the Canada forces against Ticonderoga, so as to keep Schuyler busy in that quarter; and then the army at New York, thus increased to nearly 40,000 men, might have had a fair chance of overwhelming Washington by sheer weight of numbers. Such a plan might have failed, but it is not likely that it would have led to the surrender of the British army. And if they could have disposed of Washington, the British might have succeeded. It was more necessary for them to get rid of him than to march up and down the valley of the Hudson. But it was not strange that they did not see this as we do. It is always easy enough to be wise after things have happened.

Even as it was, if their plan had really been followed, they might have succeeded. If Howe's army had gone up to meet Burgoyne, the history of the year 1777 would have been very different from what it was. We shall presently see why it did not do so. Let us now recount the fortunes of Burgoyne and St. Leger.

[Sidenote: Burgoyne takes Ticonderoga, July 5, 1777.]

Burgoyne came up Lake Champlain in June, and easily won Ticonderoga, because the Americans had failed to secure a neighbouring position which commanded the fortress. Burgoyne took Ticonderoga from Mount Defiance, just as the Americans would have taken Boston from Bunker Hill, if they had been able to stay there, just as they afterward did take it from Dorchester Heights, and just as Howe took New York after he had won Brooklyn Heights. When you have secured a position from which you can kill the enemy twice as fast as he can kill you, he must of course retire from the situation; and the sooner he goes, the better chance he has of living to fight another day. The same principle worked in all these cases, and it worked with General Howe at Harlem Heights and at White Plains.

[Sidenote: Schuyler and Gates.]

When it was known that Burgoyne had taken Ticonderoga, there was dreadful dismay in America and keen disappointment among those Whigs in England whose declared sympathies were with us. George III. was beside himself with glee, and thought that the Americans were finally defeated and disposed of. But they were all mistaken. The garrison of Ticonderoga had taken the alarm and retreated, so that Burgoyne captured only an empty fortress. He left 1000 men in charge of it, and then pressed on into the wilderness between Lake Champlain and the upper waters of the Hudson river. His real danger was now beginning to show itself, and every day it could be seen more distinctly. He was plunging into a forest, far away from all possible support from behind, and as he went on he found that there were not Tories enough in that part of the country to be of any use to him. As Burgoyne advanced, General Schuyler prudently retreated, and used up the enemy's time by breaking down bridges and putting every possible obstacle in his way. Schuyler was a rare man, thoroughly disinterested and full of sound sense; but he had many political enemies who were trying to pull him down. A large part of his army was made up of New England men, who hated him partly for the mere reason that he was a New Yorker, and partly because as such he had taken part in the long quarrel between New York and New Hampshire over the possession of the Green Mountains. The disaffection toward Schuyler was fomented by General Horatio Gates, who had for some time held command under him, but was now in Philadelphia currying favour with the delegates in Congress, especially with those from New England, in the hope of getting himself appointed to the command of the northern army in Schuyler's place. Gates was an extremely weak man, but so vain that he really believed himself equal to the highest command that Congress could be persuaded to give him. On the battle-field he seems to have been wanting even in personal courage, as he certainly was in power to handle his troops; but in society he was quite a lion. He had a smooth courteous manner and a plausible tongue which paid little heed to the difference between truth and falsehood. His lies were not very ingenious, and so they were often detected and pointed out. But while many people were disgusted by his selfishness and trickery, there were always some who insisted that he was a great genius. History can point to a good many men like General Gates. Such men sometimes shine for a while, but sooner or later they always come to be recognized as humbugs.

[Illustration: BURGOYNE'S CAMPAIGN.]

[Sidenote: Battle of Hubbardton, July 7, 1777.]

While Gates was intriguing, Schuyler was doing all in his power to impede the enemy's progress. It was on the night of July 5 that the garrison of Ticonderoga, under General St. Clair, had abandoned the fortress and retreated southward. On the 7th a battle was fought at Hubbardton between St. Clair's rear, under Seth Warner, and a portion of the British army under Fraser and Riedesel. Warner was defeated, but only after such an obstinate resistance as to check the pursuit, so that by the 12th St. Clair was able to bring his retreating troops in safety to Fort Edward, where they were united with Schuyler's army. Schuyler managed his obstructions so well that Burgoyne's utmost efforts were required to push into the wilderness at the rate of one mile per day; and meanwhile Schuyler was collecting a force of militia in the Green Mountains, under General Lincoln, to threaten Burgoyne in the rear and cut off his communications with Lake Champlain.

Burgoyne was accordingly marching into a trap, and Schuyler was doing the best that could be done. But on the first of August the intrigue against him triumphed in Congress, and Gates was appointed to supersede him in the command of the northern army. Gates, however, did not arrive upon the scene until the 19th of August, and by that time Burgoyne's situation was evidently becoming desperate.

On the last day of July Burgoyne reached Fort Edward, which Schuyler had evacuated just before. Schuyler crossed the Hudson river, and continued his retreat to Stillwater, about thirty miles above Albany. It was as far as the American retreat was to go. Burgoyne was already getting short of provisions, and before he could advance much further he needed a fresh supply of horses to drag the cannon and stores. He began to realize, when too late, that he had come far into an enemy's country. The hostile feelings of the people were roused to fury by the atrocities committed by the Indians employed in Burgoyne's army. The British supposed that the savages would prove very useful as scouts and guides, and that by offers of reward and threats of punishment they might be restrained from deeds of violence. They were very unruly, however, and apt to use the tomahawk when they found a chance.

[Sidenote: Jane McCrea.]

The sad death of Miss Jane McCrea has been described in almost as many ways as there have been people to describe it, but no one really knows how it happened. What is really known is that, on the 27th of July, while Miss McCrea was staying with her friend Mrs. McNeil, near Fort Edward, a party of Indians burst into the house and carried off both ladies. They were pursued by some American soldiers, and a few shots were exchanged. In the course of the scrimmage the party got scattered, and Mrs. McNeil was taken alone to the British camp. Next day an Indian came into the camp with Miss McCrea's scalp, which her friend recognized from its long silky hair. A search was made, and the body of the poor girl was found lying near a spring, pierced with three bullet-wounds. The Indian's story, that she was accidentally killed by a volley from the American soldiers, may well enough have been true. It is also known that she was betrothed to David Jones, a lieutenant in Burgoyne's army, and, as her own home was in New Jersey, her visit to Mrs. McNeil may very likely have been part of a plan for meeting her lover. These facts were soon woven into a story, in which Jenny was said to have been murdered while on her way to her wedding, escorted by a party of Indians whom her imprudent lover had sent to take charge of her.

[Sidenote: Battle of Bennington, Aug. 16, 1777.]

The people of the neighbouring counties, in New York and Massachusetts, enraged at the death of Miss McCrea and alarmed for the safety of their own firesides, began rising in arms. Sturdy recruits began marching to join Schuyler at Stillwater and Lincoln at Manchester in the Green Mountains. Meanwhile Burgoyne had made up his mind to attack the village of Bennington, which was Lincoln's centre of supplies. By seizing these supplies, he could get for himself what he stood sorely in need of, while at the same time the loss would cripple Lincoln and perhaps oblige him to retire from the scene. Accordingly 1000 Germans were sent out, in two detachments under colonels Baum and Breymann, to capture the village. But instead they were captured themselves. Baum was first outmanoeuvred, surrounded, and forced to surrender by John Stark, after a hot fight, in which Baum was mortally wounded. Then Breymann was put to flight and his troops dispersed by Seth Warner. Of the whole German force, 207 were killed or wounded, and at least 700 captured. Not more than 70 got back to the British camp. The American loss in killed and wounded was 56.

This brilliant victory at Bennington had important consequences. It checked Burgoyne's advance until he could get his supplies, and it decided that Lincoln's militia could get in his rear and cut off his communications with Ticonderoga. It furthermore inspired the Americans with the exulting hope that Burgoyne's whole army could be surrounded and forced to surrender.

[Sidenote: St. Leger in the Mohawk valley.]

If, however, the British had been successful in gaining the Mohawk valley and ensuring the supremacy over that region for the Tories, the fate of Burgoyne might have been averted. The Tories in that region, under Sir John Johnson and Colonel John Butler, were really formidable. As for the Indians of the Iroquois league, they had always been friendly to the English and hostile to the French; but now, when it came to making their choice between two kinds of English--the Americans and the British, they hesitated and differed in opinion. The Mohawks took sides with the British because of the friendship between Joseph Brant and the Johnsons. The Cayugas and Senecas followed on the same side; but the Onondagas, in the centre of the confederacy, remained neutral, and the Oneidas and Tuscaroras, under the influence of Samuel Kirkland and other missionaries, showed active sympathy with the Americans. It turned out, too, that the Whigs were much stronger in the valley than had been supposed.

[Sidenote: Battle of Oriskany, Aug. 6, 1777.]

After St. Leger had landed at Oswego and joined hands with his Tory and Indian allies, his entire force amounted to about 1700 men. The principal obstacle to his progress toward the Hudson river was Fort Stanwix, which stood where the city of Rome now stands. On the 3d of August St. Leger reached Fort Stanwix and laid siege to it. The place was garrisoned by 600 men under Colonel Peter Gansevoort, and the Whig yeomanry of the neighbourhood, under the heroic General Nicholas Herkimer, were on the way to relieve it, to the number of at least 800. Herkimer made an excellent plan for surprising St. Leger with an attack in the rear, while the garrison should sally forth and attack him in front. But St. Leger's Indian scouts were more nimble than Herkimer's messengers, so that he obtained his information sooner than Gansevoort. An ambush was skilfully prepared by Brant in a ravine near Oriskany, and there, on the 6th of August, was fought the most desperate and murderous battle of the Revolutionary War. It was a hand to hand fight, in which about 800 men were engaged on each side, and each lost more than one-third of its number. As the Tories and Indians were giving way, their retreat was hastened by the sounds of battle from Fort Stanwix, where the garrison was making its sally and driving back the besiegers. Herkimer remained in possession of the field at Oriskany, but his plan had been for the moment thwarted, and in the battle he had received a wound from which he died.

[Sidenote: St. Leger's flight, Aug. 22, 1777.]

Benedict Arnold had lately been sent by Washington to be of such assistance as he could to Schuyler. Arnold stood high in the confidence of both these generals. He had shown himself one of the ablest officers in the American army, he was especially skilful in getting good work out of raw troops, and he was a great favourite with his men. On hearing of the danger of Fort Stanwix, Schuyler sent him to the rescue, with 1200 men. When he was within twenty miles of that stronghold, he contrived, with the aid of some friendly Oneidas and a Tory captive whose life he spared for the purpose, to send on before him exaggerated reports of the size of his army. The device accomplished far more than he could have expected. The obstinate resistance at Oriskany had discouraged the Tories and angered the Indians. Distrust and dissension were already rife in St. Leger's camp, when such reports came in as to lead many to believe that Burgoyne had been totally defeated, and that the whole of Schuyler's army, or a great part of it, was coming up the Mohawk. This news led to riot and panic among the troops, and on August 22 St. Leger took to flight and made his way as best he could to his ships at Oswego, with scarcely the shred of an army left. This catastrophe showed how sadly mistaken the British had been in their reliance upon Tory help.

The battle of Bennington was fought on the 16th of August. Now by the overthrow of St. Leger, six days later, Burgoyne's situation had become very alarming. It was just in the midst of these events that Gates arrived, on August 19, and took command of the army at Stillwater, which was fast growing in numbers. Militia were flocking in, Arnold's force was returning, and Daniel Morgan was at hand with 500 Virginian sharpshooters. Unless Burgoyne could win a battle against overwhelming odds, there was only one thing that could save him; and that was the arrival of Howe's army at Albany, according to the ministry's programme. But Burgoyne had not yet heard a word from Howe; and Howe never came.

[Sidenote: Why Howe failed to coöperate with Burgoyne.]

This failure of Howe to coöperate with Burgoyne was no doubt the most fatal military blunder made by the British in the whole course of the war. The failure was of course unintentional on Howe's part. He meant to extend sufficient support to Burgoyne, but the trouble was that he attempted too much. He had another plan in his mind at the same time, and between the two he ended by accomplishing nothing. While he kept one eye on Albany, he kept the other on Philadelphia. He had not relished being driven back across New Jersey by Washington, and the hope of defeating that general in battle, and then pushing on to the "rebel capital" strongly tempted him. In such thoughts he was encouraged by the advice of the captive General Lee. That unscrupulous busybody felt himself in great danger, for he knew that the British regarded him in the light of a deserter from their army. While his fate was in suspense, he informed the brothers Howe that he had abandoned the American cause, and he offered them his advice and counsel for the summer campaign. This villainy of Lee's was not known till eighty years afterward, when a paper of his was discovered that revealed it in all its blackness. The Howes were sure to pay some heed to Lee's opinions, because he was supposed to have acquired a thorough knowledge of American affairs. He advised them to begin by taking Philadelphia, and supported this plan by plausible arguments. Sir William Howe seems to have thought that he could accomplish this early in the summer, and then have his hands free for whatever might be needed on the Hudson river. Accordingly on the 12th of June he started to cross the state of New Jersey with 18,000 men.

[Sidenote: Washington's masterly campaign in New Jersey, June, 1777.]

But Sir William had reckoned without his host. In a campaign of eighteen days, Washington, with only 8000 men, completely blocked the way for him, and made him give up the game. The popular histories do not have much to say about these eighteen days, because they were not marked by battles. Washington won by his marvellous skill in choosing positions where Howe could not attack him with any chance of success. Howe understood this and did not attack. He could not entice Washington into fighting at a disadvantage, and he could not march on and leave such an enemy behind without sacrificing his own communications. Accordingly on June 30 he gave up his plan and retreated to Staten Island. If there ever was a general who understood the useful art of wasting his adversary's time, Washington was that general.

Howe now decided to take his army to Philadelphia by sea. He waited a while till the news from the north seemed to show that Burgoyne was carrying everything before him; and then he thought it safe to start. He left Sir Henry Clinton in command at New York, with 7000 men, telling him to send a small force up the river to help Burgoyne, should there be any need of it, which did not then seem likely. Then he put to sea with his main force of 18,000 men, and went around to the Delaware river, which he reached at the end of July, just as Burgoyne was reaching Fort Edward.

[Sidenote: Howe's strange movement upon Philadelphia, by way of Chesapeake bay.]

Howe's next move was very strange. He afterward said that he did not go up the Delaware river, because he found that there were obstructions and forts to be passed. But he might have gone up a little way and landed his forces on the Delaware coast at a point where a single march would have brought them to Elkton, at the head of Chesapeake bay, about fifty miles southwest from Philadelphia. Instead of this, he put out to sea again and sailed four hundred miles, to the mouth of Chesapeake bay and up that bay to Elkton, where he landed his men on the 25th of August. Why he took such a roundabout course cannot be understood, unless he may have attached importance to Lee's advice that the presence of a British squadron in Chesapeake bay would help to arouse the Tories in Maryland. The British generals could not seem to make up their minds that America was a hostile country. Small blame to them, brave fellows that they were! They could not make war against America in such a fierce spirit as that in which France would now make war against Germany if she could see her way clear to do so. They were always counting on American sympathy, and this was a will-o'-the-wisp that lured them to destruction.

On landing at Elkton, Howe received orders from London, telling him to ascend the Hudson river and support Burgoyne, in any event. This order had left London in May. It was well for the Americans that the telegraph had not then been invented. Now it was the 25th of August; Burgoyne was in imminent peril; and Howe was three hundred miles away from him!

[Sidenote: Battle of the Brandywine, Sept. 11, 1777.]

All these movements had been carefully watched by Washington; and as Howe marched toward Philadelphia he found that general blocking the way at the fords of the Brandywine creek. A battle ensued on the 11th of September. It was a well-contested battle. With 11,000 men against 18,000, Washington could hardly have been expected to win a victory. He was driven from the field, but not badly defeated. He kept his army well in hand, and manoeuvred so skilfully that the British were employed for two weeks in getting over the twenty-six miles to Philadelphia.

[Sidenote: Battle of Germantown, Oct. 4, 1777.]

Before Howe had reached that city, Congress had moved away to York in Pennsylvania. When he had taken Philadelphia, he found that he could not stay there without taking the forts on the Delaware river which prevented the British ships from coming up; for by land Washington could cut off his supplies, and he could only be sure of them by water. So Howe detached part of his army to reduce these forts, leaving the rest of it at Germantown, six miles from Philadelphia. On the 4th of October, Washington attacked the force at Germantown in such a position that defeat would have quite destroyed it. The attempt failed at the critical moment because of a dense fog in which one American brigade fired into another and caused a brief panic. The forts on the Delaware were captured after hard fighting, and Washington went into winter quarters at Valley Forge.

The result of the summer's work was that, because Howe had made several mistakes and Washington had taken the utmost advantage of every one of them, the whole British plan was spoiled. Howe had used up the whole season in getting to Philadelphia, and Washington's activity had also kept Sir Henry Clinton's attention so much occupied with what was going on about the Delaware river as to prevent him from sending aid to the northward until it was too late. Sir Henry was once actually obliged to send reinforcements to Howe.

Thus Burgoyne was left to himself. He supposed that Howe was coming up the Hudson river to meet him, and so on September 13 he crossed the river and advanced to attack Gates's army, which was occupying a strong position at Bemis Heights, between Stillwater and Saratoga. It was a desperate move. While Burgoyne was making it, Lincoln's men cut his communications with Ticonderoga, so that his only hope lay in help from below; and such help never came. In this extremity he was obliged to fight on ground chosen by the Americans, because he must either fight or starve.

[Sidenote: Burgoyne is defeated by Arnold, and surrenders his army, Oct. 17, 1777.]

Under these circumstances Burgoyne fought two battles with consummate gallantry. The first was on September 19, the second on October 7. In each battle the Americans were led by Arnold and Morgan, and Gates deserves no credit for either. In both battles Arnold was the leading spirit, and in the second he was severely wounded at the moment of victory. In the first battle the British were simply repulsed, in the second they were totally defeated. This settled the fate of Burgoyne, and on the 17th of October he surrendered his whole army, now reduced to less than 6000 men, as prisoners of war. Before the final catastrophe Sir Henry Clinton had sent a small force up the river to relieve him, but it was too late. The relieving force succeeded in capturing some of the Highland forts, but turned back on hearing of Burgoyne's surrender.

CHAPTER VII. THE FRENCH ALLIANCE.

[Sidenote: Lord North changes front, and France interferes, Feb., 1778.]

This capture of a British army made more ado in Europe than anything which had happened for many a day. It was compared to Leuktra and the Caudine Fork. The immediate effect in England was to weaken the king and cause Lord North to change his policy. The tea-duty and the obnoxious acts of 1774 were repealed, the principles of colonial independence of Parliament laid down by Otis and Henry were admitted, and commissioners were sent over to America to negotiate terms of peace. It was hoped that by such ample concessions the Americans might be so appeased as to be willing to adopt some arrangement which would leave their country a part of the British Empire. As soon as the French government saw the first symptoms of such a change of policy on the part of Lord North, it decided to enter into an alliance with the United States. There was much sympathy for the Americans among educated people of all grades of society in France; but the action of the government was determined purely by hatred of England. While Great Britain and her colonies were weakening each other by war, France had up to this moment not cared to interfere. But if there was the slightest chance of a reconciliation, it was high time to prevent it; and besides, the American cause was now prosperous, and something might be made of it. The moment had come for France to seek revenge for the disasters of the Seven Years' War; and on the 6th of February, 1778, her treaty of alliance with the United States was signed at Paris.

[Sidenote: Untimely death of Lord Chatham, May 11, 1778.]

At the news of this there was an outburst of popular excitement in England. There was a strong feeling in favour of peace with America and war with France, and men of all parties united with Lord North himself in demanding that Lord Chatham, who represented such a policy, should be made prime minister. It was rightly believed that he, if any one, could both conciliate America and humiliate France. There was only one way in which Chatham could have broken the new alliance which Congress had so long been seeking. The faith of Congress was pledged to France, and the Americans would no longer hear of any terms that did not begin with the acknowledgment of their full independence. To break the alliance, it would have been necessary to concede the independence of the United States. The king felt that if he were now obliged to call Chatham to the head of affairs and allow him to form a strong ministry, it would be the end of his cherished schemes for breaking down cabinet government. There was no man whom George III. hated and feared so much as Lord Chatham. Nevertheless the pressure was so great that, but for Chatham's untimely death, the king would probably have been obliged to yield. If Chatham had lived a year longer, the war might have ended with the surrender of Burgoyne instead of continuing until the surrender of Cornwallis. As it was, Lord North consented, against his own better judgment, to remain in office and aid the king's policy as far as he could. The commissioners sent to America accomplished nothing, because they were not empowered to grant independence; and so the war went on.

[Sidenote: Change in the conduct of the war.]

There was a great change, however, in the manner in which the war was conducted. In the years 1776 and 1777 the British had pursued a definite plan for conquering New York and thus severing the connection between New England and the southern states. During the remainder of the war their only definite plan was for conquering the southern states. Their operations at the north were for the most part confined to burning and plundering expeditions along the coast in their ships, or on the frontier in connection with Tories and Indians. The war thus assumed a more cruel character. This was chiefly due to the influence of Lord George Germaine, the secretary of state for the colonies. He was a contemptible creature, weak and cruel. He had been dismissed from the army in 1759 for cowardice at the battle of Minden, and he was so generally despised that when in 1782 the king was obliged to turn him out of office and tried to console him by raising him to the peerage as Viscount Sackville, the House of Lords protested against the admission of such a creature. George III. had made this man his colonial secretary in the autumn of 1775, and he had much to do with planning the campaigns of the next two years. But now his influence in the cabinet seems to have increased. He was much more thoroughly in sympathy with the king than Lord North, who at this time was really to be pitied. Lord North would have been a fine man but for his weakness of will. He was now keeping up the war in America unwillingly, and was obliged to sanction many things of which he did not approve. In later years he bitterly repented this weakness. Now the truculent policy of Lord George Germaine began to show itself in the conduct of the war. That minister took no pains to conceal his willingness to employ Indians, to burn towns and villages, and to inflict upon the American people as much misery as possible, in the hope of breaking their spirit and tiring them out.

[Sidenote: The Conway Cabal.]

In America the first effect of Burgoyne's surrender was to strengthen a feeling of dissatisfaction with Washington, which had grown up in some quarters. In reality, as our narrative has shown, Washington had as much to do with the overthrow of Burgoyne as anybody; for if it had not been for his skilful campaign in June, 1777, Howe would have taken Philadelphia in that month, and would then have been free to assist Burgoyne. It is easy enough to understand such things afterward, but people never can see them at the time when they are happening. This is an excellent illustration of what was said at the beginning of this book, that when people are down in the midst of events they cannot see the wood because of the trees, and it is only when they have climbed the hill of history and look back over the landscape that they can see what things really meant. At the end of the year 1777 people could only see that Burgoyne had surrendered to Gates, while Washington had lost two battles and the city of Philadelphia. Accordingly there were many who supposed that Gates must be a better general than Washington, and in the army there were some discontented spirits that were only too glad to take advantage of this feeling. One of these malcontents was an Irish adventurer, Thomas Conway, who had long served in France and came over here in time to take part in the battles of Brandywine and Germantown. He had a grudge against Washington, as Charles Lee had. He thought he could get on better if Washington were out of the way. So he busied himself in organizing a kind of conspiracy against Washington, which came to be known as the "Conway Cabal." The purpose was to put forward Gates to supersede Washington, as he had lately superseded the noble Schuyler. Gates, of course, lent himself heartily to the scheme; such intrigues were what he was made for. And there were some of our noblest men who were dissatisfied with Washington, because they were ignorant of the military art, and could not understand his wonderful skill, as Frederick the Great did. Among these were John and Samuel Adams, who disapproved of "Fabian strategy." Gates and Conway tried to work upon such feelings. They hoped by thwarting and insulting Washington to wound his pride and force him to resign. In this wretched work they had altogether too much help from Congress, but they failed ignominiously because Gates's lies were too plainly discovered. The attempts to injure

Washington recoiled upon their authors. Never, perhaps, was Washington so grand as in that sorrowful winter at Valley Forge.

When the news of the French alliance arrived, in the spring of 1778, there was a general feeling of elation. People were over-confident. It seemed as if the British might be driven from the country in the course of that year. Some changes occurred in both the opposing armies. A great deal of fault was found in England with Howe and Burgoyne. The latter was allowed to go home in the spring, and took his seat in Parliament while still a prisoner on parole. He was henceforth friendly to the Americans, and opposed the further prosecution of the war. Sir William Howe resigned his command in May and went home in order to defend his conduct. Shortly before his appointment to the chief command in America, he had uttered a prophecy somewhat notable as coming from one who was about to occupy such a position. In a speech at Nottingham he had expressed the opinion that the Americans could not be subdued by any army that Great Britain could raise!

[Sidenote: Howe is superseded by Clinton.]

Howe was succeeded in the chief command by Sir Henry Clinton. His brother, Lord Howe, remained in command of the fleet until the autumn, when he was succeeded by Admiral Byron. During the winter the American army had received a very important reinforcement in the person of Baron von Steuben, an able and highly educated officer who had served on the staff of Frederick the Great. Steuben was appointed inspector-general and taught the soldiers Prussian discipline and tactics until the efficiency of the army was more than doubled. About the time of Sir William Howe's departure, Charles Lee was exchanged, and came back to his old place as senior major-general in the Continental army. Since his capture there had been a considerable falling off in his reputation, but nothing was known of his treasonable proceedings with the Howes. Probably no one in the British army knew anything about that affair except the Howes and their private secretary Sir Henry Strachey. Lee saw that the American cause was now in the ascendant, and he was as anxious as ever to supplant Washington.

[Sidenote: The Americans take the offensive; Lee's misconduct at Monmouth, June 28, 1778.]

The Americans now assumed the offensive. Count d'Estaing was approaching the coast with a powerful French fleet. Should he be able to defeat Lord Howe and get control of the Delaware river, the British army in Philadelphia would be in danger of capture. Accordingly on the 18th of June that city was evacuated by Sir Henry Clinton and occupied by Washington. As there were not enough transports to take the British army around to New York by sea, it was necessary to take the more hazardous course of marching across New Jersey. Washington pursued the enemy closely, with the view of forcing him to battle in an unfavourable situation and dealing him a fatal blow. There was some hope of effecting this, as the two armies were now about equal in size--15,000 in each--and the Americans were in excellent training. The enemy were overtaken at Monmouth Court House on the morning of June 28, but the attack was unfortunately entrusted to Lee, who disobeyed orders and made an unnecessary and shameful retreat. Washington arrived on the scene in time to turn defeat into victory. The British were driven from the field, but Lee's misconduct had broken the force of the blow which Washington had aimed at them. Lee was tried by court-martial and at first suspended from command, then expelled from the army. It was the end of his public career. He died in October, 1782.

After the battle of Monmouth the British continued their march to New York, and Washington moved his army to White Plains. Count d'Estaing arrived at Sandy Hook in July with a much larger fleet than the British had in the harbour, and a land force of 4000 men. It now seemed as if Clinton's army might be cooped up and compelled to surrender, but on examination it appeared that the largest French ships drew too much water to venture to cross the bar. All hope of capturing New York was accordingly for the present abandoned.

[Siege of Newport, Aug. 1778.]

The enemy, however, had another considerable force near at hand, besides Clinton's. Since December, 1776, they had occupied the island which gives its name to the state of Rhode Island. Its position was safe and convenient. It enabled them, if they should see fit, to threaten Boston on the one hand and the coast of Connecticut on the other, and thus to make diversions in aid of Sir Henry Clinton. The force on Rhode Island had been increased to 6000 men, under command of Sir Robert Pigott. The Americans believed that the capture of so large a force, could it be effected, would so discourage the British as to bring the war to an end; and in this belief they were very likely right. The French fleet accordingly proceeded to Newport; to the 4000 French infantry Washington added 1500 of the best of his Continentals; levies of New England yeomanry raised the total strength to 13,000; and the general command of the American troops was given to Sullivan.

The expedition was poorly managed, and failed completely. There was some delay in starting. During the first week of August the Americans landed upon the island and occupied Butts Hill. The French had begun to land on Conanicut when they learned that Lord Howe was approaching with a powerful fleet. The count then reëmbarked his men and stood out to sea, manoeuvring for a favourable position for battle. Before the fight had begun, a terrible storm scattered both fleets and damaged them severely. When D'Estaing had got his ships together again, which was not till the 20th of August, he insisted upon going to Boston for repairs, and took his infantry with him. This vexed Sullivan and disgusted the yeomanry, who forthwith dispersed and went home to look after their crops. General Pigott then tried the offensive, and attacked Sullivan in his strong position on Butts Hill, on the 29th of August. The British were defeated, but the next day Sullivan learned that Clinton was coming with heavy reinforcements, and so he was obliged to abandon the enterprise and lose no time in getting his own troops into a safe position on the mainland. In November the French fleet sailed for the West Indies, and Clinton was obliged to send 5000 men from New York to the same quarter of the world.

[Sidenote: Wyoming and Cherry Valley, July-Nov., 1778.]

In the years 1778 and 1779 the warfare on the border assumed formidable proportions. The Tories of central New York, under the Johnsons and Butlers, together with Brant and his Mohawks, made their headquarters at Fort Niagara, from which they struck frequent and terrible blows at the exposed settlements on the frontier. Early in July, 1778, a force of 1200 men, under John Butler, spread death and desolation through the beautiful valley of Wyoming in Pennsylvania. On the 10th of November, Brant and Walter Butler destroyed the village of Cherry

Valley in New York, and massacred the inhabitants. Many other dreadful things were done in the course of this year; but the affairs of Wyoming and Cherry Valley made a deeper impression than all the rest. During the following spring Washington organized an expedition of 5000 men, and sent it, under Sullivan, to lay waste the Iroquois country and capture the nest of Tory malefactors at Fort Niagara. While they were slowly advancing through the wilderness, Brant sacked the town of Minisink and destroyed a force of militia sent against him. But on the 29th of August a battle was fought on the site of the present town of Elmira, in which the Tories and Indians were defeated with great slaughter. The American army then marched through the country of the Cayugas and Senecas, and laid it waste. More than forty Indian villages were burned and all the corn was destroyed, so that the approach of winter brought famine and pestilence. Sullivan was not able to get beyond the Genesee river for want of supplies, and so Fort Niagara escaped. The Iroquois league had received a blow from which it never recovered, though for two years more their tomahawks were busy on the frontier.

[Sidenote: Conquest of the northwestern territory, 1778-79.]

At intervals during the Revolution there was more or less Indian warfare all along the border. Settlers were making their way into Kentucky and Tennessee. Feuds with these encroaching immigrants led the powerful tribe of Cherokees to take part with the British, and they made trouble enough until they were crushed by John Sevier, the "lion of the border." In 1778 Colonel Hamilton, the British commander at Detroit, attempted to stir up all the western tribes to a concerted attack upon the frontier. When the news of this reached Virginia, an expedition was sent out under George Rogers Clark, a youth of twenty-four years, to carry the war into the enemy's country. In an extremely interesting and romantic series of movements, Clark took the posts of Kaskaskia and Cahokia, on the Mississippi river, defeated and captured Colonel Hamilton at Vincennes, on the Wabash, and ended by conquering the whole northwestern territory for the state of Virginia.

[Sidenote: Storming of Stony Point, July 15, 1779.]

The year 1779 saw very little fighting in the northern states between the regular armies. The British confined themselves chiefly to marauding expeditions along the coast, from Martha's Vineyard down to the James river. These incursions were marked by cruelties unknown in the earlier part of the war. Their chief purpose would seem to have been to carry out Lord George Germaine's idea of harassing the Americans as vexatiously as possible. But in Connecticut, which perhaps suffered the worst, there was a military purpose. In July, 1779, an attack was made upon New Haven, and the towns of Fairfield and Norwalk were burned. The object was to induce Washington to weaken his force on the Hudson river by sending away troops to protect the Connecticut towns. Clinton now held the river as far up as Stony Point, and he hoped by this diversion to prepare for an attack upon Washington which, if successful, might end in the fall of West Point. If the British could get possession of West Point, it would go far toward retrieving the disaster which had befallen them at Saratoga. Washington's retort was characteristic of him. He did, as always, what the enemy did not expect. He called Anthony Wayne and asked him if he thought he could carry Stony Point by storm. Wayne replied that he could storm a very much hotter place than any known in terrestrial geography, if Washington would plan the attack. Plan and performance were equally good. At midnight of July 15 the fort was surprised and carried in a superb assault with bayonets, without the firing of a gun on the American side. It was one of the most brilliant assaults in all military history. It instantly relieved Connecticut, but Washington did not think it prudent to retain the fortress. The works were all destroyed, and the garrison, with the cannon and stores, withdrawn. The American army was as much as possible concentrated about West Point. In the general situation of affairs on the Hudson there was but little change for the next two years.

It may seem strange that so little was done in all this time. But, in fact, both England and the United States were getting exhausted, so far as the ability to carry on war was concerned.

[Sidenote: How England was weakened and hampered, 1778-81.]

As regards England, the action of France had seriously complicated the situation. England had now to protect her colonies and dependencies on the Mediterranean, in Africa, in Hindustan, and in the West Indies. In 1779 Spain declared war against her, in the hope of regaining Gibraltar and the Floridas. For three years Gibraltar was besieged by the allied French and Spanish forces. A Spanish fleet laid siege to Pensacola. France strove to regain the places which England had formerly won from her in Senegambia. War broke out in India with the Mahrattas, and with Hyder Ali of Mysore, and it required all the genius of Warren Hastings to save England's empire in Asia. We have already seen how Clinton, in the autumn of 1778, was obliged to weaken his force in New York by sending 5,000 men to the West Indies. Before the end of 1779 there were 314,000 British troops on duty in various parts of the world, but not enough could be spared for service in New York to defeat Washington's little army of 15,000. We thus begin to realize what a great event was the surrender of Burgoyne. The loss of 6,000 men by England was not in itself irreparable; but in leading to the intervention of France it was like the touching of a spring or the drawing of a bolt which sets in motion a vast system of machinery.

Under these circumstances George III. tried to form an alliance with Russia, and offered the island of Minorca as an inducement. Russia declined the offer, and such action as she took was hostile to England. It had formerly been held that the merchant ships of neutral nations, employed in trade with nations at war, might lawfully be overhauled and searched by war ships of either of the belligerent nations, and their goods confiscated. England still held this doctrine and acted upon it. But during the eighteenth century her maritime power had increased to such an extent that she could damage other nations in this way much more than they could damage her. Other nations accordingly began to maintain that goods carried in neutral ships ought to be free from seizure. Early in 1780 Denmark, Sweden, and Russia entered into an agreement known as the Armed Neutrality, by which they pledged themselves to unite in retaliating upon England whenever any of her cruisers should molest any of their ships. This league was a new source of danger to England, because it entailed the risk of war with Russia.

[Sidenote: Paul Jones, 1779.]

During these years several bold American cruisers had made the stars and stripes a familiar sight in European waters. The most famous of these cruisers, Paul Jones, made his name a terror upon the coasts of England, burned the ships in a port of Cumberland, sailed into the Frith of Forth and threatened Edinburgh, and finally captured two British war vessels off Flamborough

Head, in one of the most desperate sea-fights on record.

[Sidenote: St. Eustatius, Feb., 1781.]

Paul Jones was a regularly commissioned captain in the American navy, but because the British did not recognize Congress as a legal body they called him a pirate. When he took his prizes into a port in Holland, they requested the Dutch government to surrender him into their hands, as if he were a mere criminal to be tried at the Old Bailey. But the Dutch let him stay in port ten weeks and then depart in peace. This caused much irritation, and as there was also perpetual quarrelling over the plunder of Dutch ships by British cruisers, the two nations went to war in December, 1780. One of England's reasons for entering into this war was the desire to capture the little Dutch island of St. Eustatius in the West Indies. An immense trade was carried on there between Holland and the United States, and it was believed that the stoppage of this trade would be a staggering blow to the Americans. It was captured in February, 1781, by Admiral Rodney, private property was seized to the amount of more than twenty million dollars, and the inhabitants were treated with shameful brutality.

[Sidenote: How the Americans were weakened and hampered. The want of union.]

As England was thus fighting single-handed against France, Spain, Holland, and the United States, while the attitude of all the neutral powers was unfriendly, we can find no difficulty in understanding the weakness of her military operations in some quarters. The United States, on the other hand, found it hard to carry on the war for very different reasons. In the first place the country was really weak. The military strength of the American Union in 1780 was inferior to that of Holland, and about on a level with that of Denmark or Portugal. But furthermore the want of union made it hard to bring out such strength as there was. In the autumn of 1777 the Articles of Confederation were submitted to the several states for adoption; but the spring of 1781 had arrived before all the thirteen states had ratified them. These articles left the Continental Congress just what it was before, a mere advisory body, without power to enlist soldiers or levy taxes, without federal courts or federal officials, and with no executive head to the government. As we have already seen, the only way in which Congress could get money from the people was by requisitions upon the states, by *asking* the state-governments for it. This was always a very slow way to get money, and now the states were unusually poor. There was very little accumulated capital. Farming, fishing, ship-building, and foreign trade were the chief occupations. Farms and plantations suffered considerably from the absence of their owners in the army, and many were kept from enlisting, because it was out of the question to go and leave their families to starve. As for ship-building, fishing, and foreign trade, these occupations were almost annihilated by British cruisers. No doubt the heaviest blows that we received were thus dealt us on the water.

[Sidenote: Fall of the Continental currency:--"Not worth a Continental."]

The people were so poor that the states found it hard to collect enough revenue for their own purposes, and most of them had a way of issuing paper money of their own, which made things still worse. Under such circumstances they had very little money to give to Congress. It was necessary to borrow of France, or Spain, or Holland, and by the time these nations were all at war, that became very difficult. From the beginning of the war Congress had issued paper notes, and in 1778 the depreciation in their value was already alarming. But as soon as the exultation over Burgoyne's surrender had subsided, as soon as the hope of speedily driving out the British had been disappointed, people soon lost all confidence in the power of Congress to pay its notes, and in 1779 their value began falling with frightful rapidity. In 1780 they became worthless. It took $150 in Continental currency to buy a bushel of corn, and an ordinary suit of clothes cost $2000. Then people refused to take it, and resorted to barter, taking their pay in sheep or ploughs, in jugs of rum or kegs of salt pork, or whatever they could get. It thus became almost impossible either to pay soldiers, or to clothe and feed them properly and supply them with powder and ball. We thus see why the Americans, as well as the British conducted the war so languidly that for two years after the storming of Stony Point their main armies sat and faced each other by the Hudson river, without any movements of importance.

[Sidenote: The British conquer Georgia, 1779.]

In one quarter, however, the British began to make rapid progress. They possessed the Floridas, having got them from Spain by the treaty of 1763. Next them lay Georgia, the weakest of the thirteen states, and then came the Carolinas, with a strong Tory element in the population. For such reasons, after the great invasion of New York had failed, the British tried the plan of starting at the southern extremity of the Union and lopping off one state after another. In the autumn of 1778 General Prevost advanced from East Florida, and in a brief campaign succeeded in capturing Savannah, Sunbury, and Augusta. General Lincoln, who had won distinction in the Saratoga campaign, was appointed to command the American forces in the South. He sent General Ashe, with 1500 men, to threaten Augusta. At Ashe's approach, the British abandoned the town and retreated toward Savannah. Ashe pursued too closely and at Briar Creek, March 3, 1779, the enemy turned upon him and routed him. The Americans lost nearly 1000 men killed, wounded, and captured, besides their cannon and small arms; and this victory cost the British only 16 men killed and wounded. Augusta was reoccupied, the royal governor, Sir James Wright, was reinstated in office, and the machinery of government which had been in operation previous to 1776 was restored. Lincoln now advanced upon Augusta, but Prevost foiled him by returning the offensive and marching upon Charleston. In order to protect that city, Lincoln was obliged to retrace his steps. It was now the middle of May, and little more was done till September, when D'Estaing returned from the West Indies. On the 23d Savannah was invested by the combined forces of Lincoln and D'Estaing, and the siege was vigorously carried on for a fortnight. Then the French admiral grew impatient. On the 9th of October a fierce assault was made, in which the allies were defeated with the loss of 1000 men, including the gallant Pulaski. The French fleet then departed, and the British could look upon Georgia as recovered.

[Sidenote: And capture Charleston, with Lincoln's army, May 12, 1780.]

It was South Carolina's turn next. Washington was obliged to weaken his own force by sending most of the southern troops to Lincoln's assistance. Sir Henry Clinton then withdrew the garrisons from his advanced posts on the Hudson, and also from Rhode Island, and was thus able to leave an adequate force in New York, while he himself set sail for Savannah, December 26, 1779, with a considerable army. After the British forces were united in Georgia, they amounted to more than 13,000 men, against whom Lincoln could bring but 7000. The fate of the American army shows us what would probably have happened in New York in 1776 if an ordinary general instead of Washington had been in command. Lincoln allowed himself to be cooped up in Charleston, and after a siege of two months was obliged to surrender the city and his whole army on the 12th of May, 1780. This was the most serious disaster the Americans had suffered since the loss of Fort Washington. The dashing cavalry leader, Tarleton, soon cut to pieces whatever remnants of their army were left in South Carolina. Sir Henry Clinton returned in June to New York, leaving Lord Cornwallis with 5000 men to carry on the work. The Tories, thus supported, got the upperhand in the interior of the state, which suffered from all the horrors of civil war. The American cause was sustained only by partisan leaders, of whom the most famous were Francis Marion and Thomas Sumter.

[Sidenote: Battle of Camden, Aug. 16, 1780.]

When the news of Lincoln's surrender reached the North, the emergency was felt to be desperate. A fresh army was raised, consisting of about 2000 superbly trained veterans of the Maryland and Delaware lines, under the Baron de Kalb, and such militia as could be raised in Virginia and North Carolina. The chief command was given to Gates, whose conduct from the start was a series of blunders. The most important strategic point in South Carolina was Camden, at the intersection of the principal roads from the coast to the mountains and from north to south. In marching upon this point Gates was met by Lord Cornwallis on the 16th of August and utterly routed. Kalb was mortally wounded at the head of the Maryland troops, who held their ground nobly till overwhelmed by numbers; the Delaware men were cut to pieces; the militia were swept away in flight, and Gates with them. His northern laurels, as it was said, had changed into southern willows; and for the second time within three months an American army at the South had been annihilated.

This was, on the whole, the darkest moment of the war. For a moment in July there had been a glimmer of hopefulness when the Count de Rochambeau arrived with 6000 men who were landed on Rhode Island. The British fleet, however, soon came and blockaded them there, and again the hearts of the people were sickened with hope deferred. It seemed as if Lord George Germaine's policy of "tiring the Americans out" might be going to succeed after all. When the value of the Continental paper money now fell to zero, it was a fair indication that the people had pretty much lost all faith in Congress. In the army the cases of desertion to the British lines averaged about a hundred per month.

[Sidenote: Benedict Arnold's treason, July-Sept., 1780.]

This was a time when a man of bold and impulsive temperament, prone to cherish romantic schemes, smarting under an accumulation of injuries, and weak in moral principle, might easily take it into his head that the American cause was lost, and that he had better carve out a new career for himself, while wreaking vengeance on his enemies. Such seems to have been the case with Benedict Arnold. He had a great and well-earned reputation for skill and bravery. His military services up to the time of Burgoyne's surrender had been of priceless value, and he had always stood high in Washington's favour. But he had a genius for getting into quarrels, and there seem always to have been people who doubted his moral soundness. At the same time he had good reason to complain of the treatment which he received from Congress. The party hostile to Washington sometimes liked to strike at him in the persons of his favourite generals, and such admirable men as Greene and Morgan had to bear the brunt of this ill feeling. Early in 1777 five brigadier generals junior to Arnold in rank and vastly inferior to him in ability and reputation had been promoted over him to the grade of major-general. On this occasion he had shown an excellent spirit, and when sent by Washington to the aid of Schuyler, he had signified his willingness to serve under St. Clair and Lincoln, two of the juniors who had been raised above him. Arnold was a warm friend to Schuyler, and perhaps did not take enough pains to conceal his poor opinion of Gates. Other officers in the northern army let it plainly be seen that they placed more confidence in Arnold than in Gates, and the result was a bitter quarrel between the two generals, echoes of which were probably afterwards heard in Congress.

If Arnold's wound on the field of Saratoga had been a mortal wound, he would have been ranked, among the military heroes of the Revolution, next to Washington and Greene. Perhaps, however, in a far worse sense than is commonly conveyed by the term, it proved to be his death-wound, for it led to his being placed in command of Philadelphia. He was assigned to that position because his wounded leg made him unfit for active service. Congress had restored him to his relative rank, but now he soon got into trouble with the state government of Pennsylvania. It is not easy to determine how much ground there may have been for the charges brought against him early in 1779 by the state government. One of them concerned his personal honesty, the others were so trivial in character as to make the whole affair look somewhat like a case of persecution. They were twice investigated, once by a committee of Congress and once by a court-martial. On the serious charge, which affected his pecuniary integrity, he was acquitted; on two of the trivial charges, of imprudence in the use of some public wagons, and of carelessness in granting a pass for a ship, he was convicted and sentenced to be reprimanded. The language in which Washington couched the reprimand showed his feeling that Arnold was too harshly dealt with.

If the matter had stopped here, posterity would probably have shared Washington's feeling. But the government of Pennsylvania must have had stronger grounds for distrust of Arnold than it was able to put into the form of definite charges. Soon after his arrival in Philadelphia he fell in love with a beautiful Tory lady, to whom he was presently married. He was thus thrown much into the society of Tories and was no doubt influenced by their views. He had for some time considered himself ill-treated, and at first thought of leaving the service and settling upon a grant of land in western New York. Then, as the charges against him were pressed and his anger increased, he seems to have dallied with the notion of going over to the British. At length in the early summer of 1780, after the reprimand, his treasonable purpose seems to have taken definite shape. As General Monk in 1660 decided that the only way to restore peace in England was to desert the cause of the Commonwealth and bring back Charles II., so Arnold seems now to have thought that the cause of American independence was ruined, and that the best prospect for a career for himself lay in deserting it and helping to bring back the rule of George III. In this period of general depression, when even the unconquerable Washington said "I have almost ceased to hope," one staggering blow would be very likely to end the struggle. There could be no heavier blow than the loss of the Hudson river, and with baseness almost incredible Arnold asked for the command of West Point, with the intention of betraying it into the hands of Sir Henry Clinton. The depth of his villainy on this occasion makes it probable that there were good grounds for the suspicions with which some people had for a long time regarded him, although

Washington, by putting him in command of the most important position in the country, showed that his own confidence in him was unabated. The successful execution of the plot seemed to call for a personal interview between Arnold and Clinton's adjutant-general, Major John André, who was entrusted with the negotiation. Such a secret interview was extremely difficult to bring about, but it was effected on the 21st of September, 1780. After a marvellous chapter of accidents, André was captured just before reaching the British lines. But for his hasty and quite unnecessary confession that he was a British officer, which led to his being searched, the plot would in all probability have been successful. The papers found on his person, which left no room for doubt as to the nature of the black scheme, were sent to Washington; the principal traitor, forewarned just in the nick of time, escaped to the British at New York; and Major André was condemned as a spy and hanged on the 2d of October.

[Sidenote: Battle of King's Mountain, Oct. 7, 1780.]

Only five days after the execution of André an event occurred at the South which greatly relieved the prevailing gloom of the situation. It was the first of a series of victories which were soon to show that the darkness of 1780 was the darkness that comes before dawn. After his victory at Camden, Lord Cornwallis found it necessary to give his army some rest from the intense August heat. In September he advanced into North Carolina, boasting that he would soon conquer all the states south of the Susquehanna river. But his line of march now lay far inland, and the British armies were never able to accomplish much except in the neighbourhood of their ships, where they could be reasonably sure of supplies. In traversing Mecklenburg county Cornwallis soon found himself in a very hostile and dangerous region, where there were no Tories to befriend him. One of his best partisan commanders, Major Ferguson, penetrated too far into the mountains. The backwoodsmen of Tennessee and Kentucky, the Carolinas, and western Virginia were aroused; and under their superb partisan leaders--Shelby, Sevier, Cleaveland, McDowell, Campbell, and Williams--gave chase to Ferguson, who took refuge upon what he deemed an impregnable position on the top of King's Mountain. On the 7th of October the backwoodsmen stormed the mountain, Ferguson was shot through the heart, 400 of his men were killed and wounded, and all the rest, 700 in number, surrendered at discretion. The Americans lost 28 killed and 60 wounded. There were some points in this battle, which remind one of the British defeat at Majuba Hill in southern Africa in 1881.

In the series of events which led to the surrender of Cornwallis, the battle of King's Mountain played a part similar to that played by the battle of Bennington in the series of events which led to the surrender of Burgoyne. It was the enemy's first serious disaster, and its immediate result was to check his progress until the Americans could muster strength enough to overthrow him. The events, however, were much more complicated in Cornwallis's case, and took much longer to unfold themselves. Burgoyne surrendered within nine anxious weeks after Bennington; Cornwallis maintained himself, sometimes with fair hopes of final victory, for a whole year after King's Mountain.

[Illustration]

[Sidenote: Greene takes command in South Carolina, Dec. 2, 1780.]

As soon as he heard the news of the disaster he fell back to Winnsborough, in South Carolina, and called for reinforcements. While they were arriving, the American army, recruited and reorganized since its crushing defeat at Camden, advanced into Mecklenburg county. Gates was superseded by Greene, who arrived upon the scene on the 2d of December. Under Greene were three Virginians of remarkable ability,--Daniel Morgan; William Washington, who was a distant cousin of the commander-in-chief; and Henry Lee, familiarly known as "Light-horse Harry," father of the great general, Robert Edward Lee. The little army numbered only 2000 men, but a considerable part of them were disciplined veterans fully a match for the British infantry.

In order to raise troops in Virginia to increase this little force, Steuben was sent down to that state. In order to interfere with such recruiting, and to make diversions in aid of Cornwallis, detachments from the British army were also sent by sea from New York to Virginia. The first of these detachments, under General Leslie, had been obliged to keep on to South Carolina, to make good the loss inflicted upon Cornwallis at King's Mountain. To replace Leslie in Virginia, the traitor Arnold was sent down from New York. The presence of these subsidiary forces in Virginia was soon to influence in a decisive way the course of events.

[Sidenote: Battle of the Cowpens, Jan. 17, 1781.]

Greene, on reaching South Carolina, acted with boldness and originality. He divided his little army into two bodies, one of which coöperated with Marion's partisans in the northeastern part of the state, and threatened Cornwallis's communications with the coast. The other body he sent under Morgan to the southwestward, to threaten the inland posts and their garrisons. Thus worried on both flanks, Cornwallis presently divided his own force, sending Tarleton with 1100 men, to dispose of Morgan. Tarleton came up with Morgan on the 17th of January, 1781, at a grazing-ground known as the Cowpens, not far from King's Mountain. The battle which ensued was well fought, and on Morgan's part it was a wonderful piece of tactics. With only 900 men in open field he surrounded and nearly annihilated a superior force. The British lost 230 in killed and wounded, 600 prisoners, and all their guns. Tarleton escaped with 270 men. The Americans lost 12 killed and 61 wounded.

[Sidenote: Battle of Guilford, March 15, 1781.]

The two battles, King's Mountain and the Cowpens, deprived Cornwallis of nearly all his light-armed troops, and he was just entering upon a game where swiftness was especially required. It was his object to intercept Morgan and defeat him before he could effect a junction with the other part of the American army. It was Greene's object to march the two parts of his army in converging directions northward across North Carolina and unite them in spite of Cornwallis. By moving in this direction Greene was always getting nearer to his reinforcements from Virginia, while Cornwallis was always getting further from his supports in South Carolina. It was brilliant strategy on Greene's part, and entirely successful. Cornwallis had to throw away a great deal of his baggage and otherwise weaken himself, but in spite of all he could do, he was outmarched. The two wings of the American army came together and were joined by the reinforcements; so that at Guilford Court House, on the 15th of March, Cornwallis found himself obliged to fight against heavy odds, two hundred miles from the coast and almost as far from the nearest point in South Carolina at which he could get support.

The battle of Guilford was admirably managed by both commanders and stubbornly fought by the troops. At nightfall the British held the field, with the loss of nearly one third of their number, and the Americans were repulsed. But Cornwallis could not stay in such a place, and could not afford to risk another battle. There was nothing for him to do but retreat to Wilmington, the nearest point on the coast. There he stopped and pondered.

[Sidenote: Cornwallis retreats into Virginia.]

His own force was sadly depleted, but he knew that Arnold in Virginia was being heavily reinforced from New York. The only safe course seemed to march northward and join in the operations in Virginia; then afterwards to return southward. This course Cornwallis pursued, arriving at Petersburg and taking command of the troops there on the 20th of May.

[Sidenote: Greene takes Camden, May 10, 1781.]

[Sidenote: Battle of Eutaw Springs, Sept. 8, 1781.]

Meanwhile Greene, after pursuing Cornwallis for about fifty miles from Guilford, faced about and marched with all speed upon Camden, a hundred and sixty miles distant. Whatever his adversary might do, he was now going to seize the great prize of the campaign, and break the enemy's hold upon South Carolina. Lord Rawdon held Camden. Greene stopped at Hobkirk's Hill, two miles to the north, and sent Marion and Lee to take Fort Watson, and thus cut the enemy's communications with the coast. On April 23 Fort Watson surrendered; on the 25th Rawdon defeated Greene at Hobkirk's Hill, but as his communications were cut, the victory did him no good. He was obliged to retreat toward the coast, and Greene took Camden on the 10th of May. Having thus obtained the commanding point, Greene went on until he had reduced every one of the inland posts. At last on the 8th of September he fought an obstinate battle at Eutaw Springs, in which both sides claimed the victory. The facts were that he drove the British from their first position, but they rallied upon a second position from which he failed to drive them. Here, however, as always after one of Greene's battles, it was the enemy who retreated and he who pursued. His strategy never failed. After Eutaw Springs the British remained shut up in Charleston under cover of their ships, and the American government was reëstablished over South Carolina. Among all the campaigns in history that have been conducted with small armies, there have been few, if any, more brilliant than Greene's.

[Sidenote: Lafayette and Cornwallis in Virginia, May-Sept., 1718.]

There was something especially piquant in the way in which after Guilford he left Cornwallis to himself. It reminds one of a chess-player who first gets the queen off the board, where she can do no harm, and then wins the game against the smaller pieces. As for Cornwallis, when he reached Petersburg, May 20, he found himself at the head of 5000 men. Arnold had just been recalled to New York, and Lafayette, who had been sent down to oppose him, was at Richmond with 3000 men. A campaign of nine weeks ensued, in the first part of which Cornwallis tried to catch Lafayette and bring him to battle. The general movement was from Richmond up to Fredericksburg, then over toward Charlottesville, then back to the James river, then down the north bank of the river. But during the last part the tables were turned, and it was Lafayette, reinforced by Wayne and Steuben, that pursued Cornwallis on his retreat to the coast. At the end of July the British general reached Yorktown, where he was reinforced and waited with 7000 men.

[Sidenote: Washington's masterly movement.]

We may now change our simile, and liken Cornwallis to a ball between two bats. The first bat, which had knocked him up into Virginia, was Greene; the second, which sent him quite out of the game, was Washington. The remarkable movement which the latter general now proceeded to execute would have been impossible without French coöperation. A French fleet of overwhelming power, under the Count de Grasse, was approaching Chesapeake bay. Washington, in readiness for it, had first moved Rochambeau's army from Rhode Island across Connecticut to the Hudson river. Then, as soon as all the elements of the situation were disclosed, he left part of his force in position on the Hudson, and in a superb march led the rest down to Virginia. Sir Henry Clinton at New York was completely hoodwinked. He feared that the real aim of the French fleet was New York, in which case it would be natural that an American land-force should meet it at Staten island. Now a glance at the map of New Jersey will show that Washington's army, starting from West Point, could march more than half the way toward Philadelphia and still be supposed to be aiming at Staten island. Washington was a master hand for secrecy. When his movement was first disclosed, his own generals, as well as Sir Henry Clinton, took it for granted that Staten island was the point aimed at. It was not until he had passed Philadelphia that Clinton began to surmise that he might be going down to Virginia.

When this fact at length dawned upon the British commander, he made a futile attempt at a diversion by sending Benedict Arnold to attack New London. It was as weak as the act of a drowning man who catches at a straw. Arnold's expedition, cruel and useless as it was, crowned his infamy. A sad plight for a man of his power! If he had only had more strength of character, he might now have been marching with his old friend Washington to victory. With this wretched affair at New London, the brilliant and wicked Benedict Arnold disappears from American history. He died in London, in 1801, a broken-hearted and penitent man, as his grandchildren tell us, praying God with his last breath to forgive his awful crime.

[Sidenote: Surrender of Cornwallis at Yorktown, Oct. 19, 1781.]

Washington's march was so swift and so cunningly planned that nothing could check it. On the 26th of September the situation was complete. Washington had added his force to that of Lafayette, so that 16,000 men blockaded Cornwallis upon the Yorktown peninsula. The great French fleet, commanding the waters about Chesapeake bay, closed in behind and prevented escape. It was a very unusual thing for the French thus to get control of the water and defy the British on their own element. It was Washington's unwearied vigilance that, after waiting long for such a chance, had seized it without a moment's delay. As soon as Cornwallis was thus caught between a hostile army and a hostile fleet, the problem was solved. On the 19th of October the British army surrendered. Washington presently marched his army back to the Hudson and made his headquarters at Newburgh.

[Sidenote: Overthrow of George III.'s political schemes, May, 1784.]

When Lord North at his office in London heard the dismal news, he walked up and down the room, wringing his hands and crying, "O God, it is all over!" Yorktown was indeed decisive. In the course of the winter the British lost Georgia. The embers of Indian warfare still smouldered on the border, but the great War for Independence was really at an end. The king's friends had for some time been losing strength in England, and Yorktown completed their defeat. In March, 1782, Lord North's ministry resigned. A succession of short-lived ministries followed; first, Lord Rockingham's, until July, 1782; then Lord Shelburne's, until February, 1783; then, after five weeks without a government, there came into power the strange Coalition between Fox and North, from April to December. During these two years the king was trying to intrigue with one interest against another so as to maintain his own personal government. With this end in view he tried the bold experiment of dismissing the Coalition and making the young William Pitt prime minister, without a majority in Parliament. After a fierce constitutional struggle, which lasted all winter, Pitt dissolved Parliament, and in the new election in May, 1784, obtained the greatest majority ever given to an English minister. But the victory was Pitt's and the people's, not the king's. This election of 1784 overthrew all the cherished plans of George III. in pursuance of which he had driven the American colonies into rebellion. It established cabinet government more firmly than ever, so that for the next seventeen years the real ruler of Great Britain was William Pitt.

CHAPTER VIII.BIRTH OF THE NATION.

[Sidenote: The treaty of peace, 1782-83.]

The year 1782 was marked by great victories for the British in the West Indies and at Gibraltar. But they did not alter the situation in America. The treaty of peace by which Great Britain acknowledged the independence of the United States was made under Lord Shelburne's ministry in the autumn of 1782, and adopted and signed by the Coalition on the 3d of September, 1783. The negotiations were carried on at Paris by Franklin, Jay, and John Adams, on the part of the Americans; and they won a diplomatic victory in securing for the United States the country between the Alleghany mountains and the Mississippi river. This was done against the wishes of the French government, which did not wish to see the United States become too powerful. At the same time Spain recovered Minorca and the Floridas. France got very little except the satisfaction of having helped in diminishing the British empire.

[Sidenote: Troubles with the army, 1781-83.]

The return of peace did not bring contentment to the Americans. Because Congress had no means of raising a revenue or enforcing its decrees, it was unable to make itself respected either at home or abroad. For want of pay the army became very troublesome. In January, 1781, there had been a mutiny of Pennsylvania and New Jersey troops which at one moment looked very serious. In the spring of 1782 some of the officers, disgusted with the want of efficiency in the government, seem to have entertained a scheme for making Washington king; but Washington met the suggestion with a stern rebuke. In March, 1783, inflammatory appeals were made to the officers at the headquarters of the army at Newburgh. It seems to have been intended that the army should overawe Congress and seize upon the government until the delinquent states should contribute the money needed for satisfying the soldiers and other public creditors. Gates either originated this scheme or willingly lent himself to it, but an eloquent speech from Washington prevailed upon the officers to reject and condemn it.

On the 19th of April, 1783, the eighth anniversary of Lexington, the cessation of hostilities was formally proclaimed, and the soldiers were allowed to go home on furloughs. The army was virtually disbanded. There were some who thought that this ought not to be done while the British forces still remained in New York; but Congress was afraid of the army and quite ready to see it scattered. On the 21st of June Congress was driven from Philadelphia by a small band of drunken soldiers clamorous for pay. It was impossible for Congress to get money. Of the Continental taxes assessed in 1783, only one fifth part had been paid by the middle of 1785. After peace was made, France had no longer any end to gain by lending us money, and European bankers, as well as European governments, regarded American credit as dead.

[Sidenote: Congress unable to fulfil the treaty.]

There was a double provision of the treaty which could not be carried out because of the weakness of Congress. It had been agreed that Congress should request the state governments to repeal various laws which they had made from time to time confiscating the property of Tories and hindering the collection of private debts due from American to British merchants. Congress did make such a request, but it was not heeded. The laws hindering the payment of debts were not repealed; and as for the Tories, they were so badly treated that between 1783 and 1785 more than 100,000 left the country. Those from the southern states went mostly to Florida and the Bahamas; those from the north made the beginnings of the Canadian states of Ontario and New Brunswick. A good many of them were reimbursed for their losses by Parliament.

[Sidenote: Great Britain retaliates, presuming upon the weakness of the feeling of union among the states.]

When the British government saw that these provisions of the treaty were not fulfilled, it retaliated by refusing to withdraw its troops from the northern and western frontier posts. The British army sailed from Charleston on the 14th of December, 1782, and from New York on the 25th of November, 1783, but in contravention of the treaty small garrisons remained at Ogdensburgh, Oswego, Niagara, Erie, Sandusky, Detroit, and Mackinaw until the 1st of June, 1796. Besides this, laws were passed which bore very severely upon American commerce, and the Americans found it impossible to retaliate because the different states would not agree upon any commercial policy in common. On the other hand, the states began making commercial war upon each other, with navigation laws and high tariffs. Such laws were passed by New York to interfere with the trade of Connecticut, and the merchants of the latter state began to hold meetings and pass resolutions forbidding all trade whatever with New York.

The old quarrels about territory were kept up, and in 1784 the troubles in Wyoming and in the Green Mountains came to the very verge of civil war. People in Europe, hearing of such things, believed that the Union would soon fall to pieces and become the prey of foreign powers. It was disorder and calamity of this sort that such men as Hutchinson had feared, in case the control of Great Britain over the colonies should cease. George III. looked upon it all with satisfaction, and believed that before long the states would one after another become repentant and beg to be taken back into the British empire.

[Sidenote: The craze for paper money and the Shays rebellion, 1786.]

The troubles reached their climax in 1786. Because there seemed to be no other way of getting money, the different states began to issue their promissory notes, and then tried to compel people by law to receive such notes as money. There was a strong "paper money" party in all the states except Connecticut and Delaware. The most serious trouble was in Rhode Island and Massachusetts. In both states the farmers had been much impoverished by the war. Many farms were mortgaged, and now and then one was sold to satisfy creditors. The farmers accordingly clamoured for paper money, but the merchants in towns like Boston or Providence, understanding more about commerce, were opposed to any such miserable makeshifts. In Rhode Island the farmers prevailed. Paper money was issued, and harsh laws were passed against all who should refuse to take it at its face value. The merchants refused, and in the towns nearly all business was stopped during the summer of 1786.

In the Massachusetts legislature the paper money party was defeated. There was a great outcry among the farmers against merchants and lawyers, and some were heard to maintain that the time had come for wiping out all debts. In August, 1786, the malcontents rose in rebellion, headed by one Daniel Shays, who had been a captain in the Continental army. They began by trying to prevent the courts from sitting, and went on to burn barns, plunder houses, and attack the arsenal at Springfield. The state troops were called out, under General Lincoln, two or three skirmishes were fought, in which a few lives were lost, and at length in February, 1787, the insurrection was suppressed.

[Sidenote: The Mississippi question, 1786.]

At that time the mouth of the Mississippi river and the country on its western bank belonged to Spain. Kentucky and Tennessee were rapidly becoming settled by people from Virginia and North Carolina, and these settlers wished to trade with New Orleans. The Spanish government was unfriendly and wished to prevent such traffic. The people of New England felt little interest in the southwestern country or the Mississippi river, but were very anxious to make a commercial treaty with Spain. The government of Spain refused to make such a treaty except on condition that American vessels should not be allowed to descend the Mississippi river below the mouth of the Yazoo. When Congress seemed on the point of yielding to this demand, the southern states were very angry. The New England states were equally angry at what they called the obstinacy of the South, and threats of secession were heard on both sides.

[Sidenote: The northwestern territory; the first national domain, 1780-87.]

Perhaps the only thing that kept the Union from falling to pieces in 1786 was the Northwestern Territory, which George Rogers Clark had conquered in 1779, and which skilful diplomacy had enabled us to keep when the treaty was drawn up in 1782. Virginia claimed this territory and actually held it, but New York, Massachusetts, and Connecticut also had claims upon it. It was the idea of Maryland that such a vast region ought not to be added to any one state, or divided between two or three of the states, but ought to be the common property of the Union. Maryland had refused to ratify the Articles of Confederation until the four states that claimed the northwestern territory should yield their claims to the United States. This was done between

1780 and 1785, and thus for the first time the United States government was put in possession of valuable property which could be made to yield an income and pay debts. This piece of property was about the first thing in which all the American people were alike interested, after they had won their independence. It could be opened to immigration and made to pay the whole cost of the war and much more. During these troubled years Congress was busy with plans for organizing this territory, which at length resulted in the famous Ordinance of 1787 laying down fundamental laws for the government of what has since developed into the five great states of Ohio, Indiana, Illinois, Michigan, and Wisconsin. While other questions tended to break up the Union, the questions that arose in connection with this work tended to hold it together.

[Sidenote: The convention at Annapolis, Sept. 11, 1786.]

The need for easy means of communication between the old Atlantic states and this new country behind the mountains led to schemes which ripened in course of time into the construction of the Chesapeake and Ohio and the Erie canals. In discussing such schemes, Maryland and Virginia found it necessary to agree upon some kind of commercial policy to be pursued by both states. Then it was thought best to seize the occasion for calling a general convention of the states to decide upon a uniform system of regulations for commerce. This convention was held at Annapolis in September, 1786, but only five states had sent delegates, and so the convention adjourned after adopting an address written by Alexander Hamilton, calling for another convention to meet at Philadelphia on the second Monday of the following May, "to devise such further provisions as shall appear necessary to render the constitution of the federal government adequate to the exigencies of the Union."

The Shays rebellion and the quarrel about the Mississippi river had by this time alarmed people so that it began to be generally admitted that the federal government must be in some way strengthened. If there were any doubt as to this, it was removed by the action of New York. An amendment to the Articles of Confederation had been proposed, giving Congress the power of levying customs-duties and appointing the collectors. By the summer of 1786 all the states except New York had consented to this. But in order to amend the articles, unanimous consent was necessary, and in February, 1787, New York's refusal defeated the amendment. Congress was thus left without any immediate means of raising a revenue, and it became quite clear that something must be done without delay.

[Sidenote: The Federal Convention at Philadelphia, May-Sept., 1787.]

The famous Federal Convention met at Philadelphia in May, 1787, and remained in session four months, with Washington presiding. Its work was the framing of the government under which we are now living, and in which the evils of the old confederation have been avoided. The trouble had all the while been how to get the whole American people *represented* in some body that could thus rightfully *tax* the whole American people. This was the question which the Albany Congress had tried to settle in 1754, and which the Federal Convention did settle in 1787.

In the old confederation, starting with the Continental Congress in 1774, the government was all vested in a single body which represented states, but did not represent individual persons. It was for that reason that it was called a congress rather than a parliament. It was more like a congress of European states than the legislative body of a nation, such as the English parliament was. It had no executive and no judiciary. It could not tax, and it could not enforce its decrees.

[Sidenote: The new government, in which the Revolution was consummated, 1789.]

The new constitution changed all this by creating the House of Representatives which stood in the same relation to the whole American people as the legislative assembly of each single state to the people of that state. In this body the people were represented, and could therefore tax themselves. At the same time in the Senate the old equality between the states was preserved. All control over commerce, currency, and finance was lodged in this new Congress, and absolute free trade was established between the states. In the office of President a strong executive was created. And besides all this there was a system of federal courts for deciding questions arising under federal laws. Most remarkable of all, in some respects, was the power given to the federal Supreme Court, of deciding, in special cases, whether laws passed by the several states, or by Congress itself, were conformable to the Federal Constitution.

Many men of great and various powers played important parts in effecting this change of government which at length established the American Union in such a form that it could endure; but the three who stood foremost in the work were George Washington, James Madison, and Alexander Hamilton. Two other men, whose most important work came somewhat later, must be mentioned along with these, for the sake of completeness. It was John Marshall, chief justice of the United States from 1801 to 1835, whose profound decisions did more than those of any later judge could ever do toward establishing the sense in which the Constitution must be understood. It was Thomas Jefferson, president of the United States from 1801 to 1809, whose sound democratic instincts and robust political philosophy prevented the federal government from becoming too closely allied with the interests of particular classes, and helped to make it what it should be,--a "government of the people, by the people, and for the people." In the *making* of the government under which we live, these five names--Washington, Madison, Hamilton, Jefferson, and Marshall--stand before all others. I mention them here chronologically, in the order of the times at which their influence was felt at its maximum.

When the work of the Federal Convention was sanctioned by the Continental Congress and laid before the people of the several states, to be ratified by special conventions in each state, there was earnest and sometimes bitter discussion. Many people feared that the new government would soon degenerate into a tyranny. But the century and a half of American history that had already elapsed had afforded such noble political training for the people that the discussion was, on the whole, more reasonable and more fruitful than any that had ever before been undertaken by so many men. The result was the adoption of the Federal Constitution, followed by the inauguration of George Washington, on the 30th of April, 1789, as President of the United States. And with this event our brief story may fitly end.

12899021R00045

Printed in Great Britain
by Amazon.co.uk, Ltd.,
Marston Gate.